Character Counts

Os Guinness is an author of numerous books and a speaker of international renown. Born in China and educated in England, he is a graduate of Oxford University. Dr. Guinness has lived in the United States since 1984 and has been a visiting fellow at the Brookings Institution. He is currently senior fellow of The Trinity Forum, an "academy without walls" that engages the leading ideas of our day in the context of faith. He resides in McLean, Virginia.

Also by Os Guinness

The American Hour: A Time of Reckoning and the Once and Future Role of Faith

The Call: Finding and Fulfilling the Central Purpose of Your Life

Dining with the Devil: The Megachurch Movement Flirts with Modernity

The Dust of Death: The Sixties Counterculture and How It Changed America Forever

Fit Bodies, Fat Minds: Why Evangelicals Don't Think and What to Do about It

God in the Dark: The Assurance of Faith beyond a Shadow of Doubt

Invitation to the Classics, coeditor

Character Counts

Leadership Qualities
in Washington, Wilberforce,
Lincoln, and Solzhenitsyn

Os Guinness, editor

Baker Books
A Division of Baker Book House Co
Grand Rapids, Michigan 49516

Published by Baker Books
a division of Baker Book House Company
P.O. Box 6287, Grand Rapids, MI 49516-6287

Third printing, October 1999

Printed in the United States of America

Library of Congress Cataloging-in-Publication Data

Character counts : leadership qualities in Washington, Wilberforce, Lincoln, and
  Solzhenitsyn / Os Guinness, editor.
    p.   cm.
  ISBN 0-8010-5824-4 (paper)
  1. Christian biography. 2. Washington, George, 1732–1799. 3. Wilberforce,
William, 1759–1833. 4. Lincoln, Abraham, 1809–1865. 5. Solzhenitsyn,
Aleksandr Isayevich, 1918– . 6. Character—Case studies. I. Guinness, Os.
BR1702.C48 1999
270.8′092′2—dc21   98-44191

The section written by Paul F. Boller is taken from *George Washington and Religion* (Dallas: SMU Press, 1963) and is reprinted with permission.

Excerpts from "Abraham Lincoln: Theologian of American Anguish" by David Elton Trueblood is copyright © 1973 by David Elton Trueblood. Reprinted with permission of HarperCollins Publishers, Inc.

Excerpts from *The Oak and the Calf* by Aleksandr I. Solzhenitsyn is copyright © 1975 by Aleksandr I. Solzhenitsyn. English translation © 1979, 1980 by Harper & Row Publishers, Inc. Reprinted by permission of HarperCollins Publishers, Inc.

For information about academic books, resources for Christian leaders, and all new releases available from Baker Book House, visit our web site:
http://www.bakerbooks.com

Liberty cannot be preserved without general knowledge among the people who have the right to that knowledge and the desire to know. But besides this, they have a right, an indisputable, unalienable, indefeasible, divine right to that most dreaded and envied kind of knowledge—I mean of the character and conduct of their rulers.

JOHN ADAMS

One of the troubles of our time is that we are all, I think, precocious as personalities and backward as characters.

W. H. AUDEN

In the White House, character and personality are extremely important because there are no other limitations. . . . Restraint must come from within the presidential soul and prudence from within the presidential mind. The adversary forces which temper the actions of others do not come into play until it is too late to change course.

GEORGE REEDY, SPECIAL ASSISTANT TO LBJ

In a president, character is everything. A president doesn't have to be brilliant. . . . He doesn't have to be clever; you can hire clever. White Houses are always full of quick-witted people with ready advice on how to flip a senator or implement a strategy. . . . But you can't buy courage and decency; you can't rent a strong moral sense. A president must bring those things with him.

PEGGY NOONAN, SPEECHWRITER FOR RONALD REAGAN

Contents

Introduction

Os Guinness

"If President Clinton did not exist, he would have to be invented." Or to express the point more carefully, the recent crisis of America's first postmodern president is not just the sad story of a flawed individual, but the full flowering of a generation of trends in American society. "There but for the grace of God . . ." is always true for all of us as individuals. But today the path toward temptation is rarely lonely. Egged on by pop-prophets and trendsetters of all kinds, we are apt to be lured down it in the company of a cohort of our peers, all stepping out fearlessly to the beat of the drummers of our time.

So it is that recent events in Washington have at last raised a warning flag, but the damage is already done. In large parts of American life character in leadership has been replaced by image, truth by power and plausibility, and confession and moral changes by spin control and image makeovers. Having sown the seeds, we can begin to survey our harvest.

Clearly, for followers of Christ and for all who appreciate the Jewish and Christian roots of our Western civilization, there is work to be done and thinking to be thought.

The trends of several generations cannot be protested out of existence in five minutes—especially where we face a double problem. Various parts of the foundation of our civilization have not only been assaulted by certain critics but have grown hollow even to their guardians. Character in leadership is such a point.

At the end of the twentieth century one of the most urgent items of unfinished business for the new millennium is the issue of leadership in free societies—and in particular the place of character in leadership. "Character counts," its proponents say. "Character has consequences." "Nonsense," reply the critics. "In the modern world competence and charisma matter more than character."

It doesn't take a cynic to point out that today's concern with character is often negative or patronizing. In political attack ads, for instance, purported champions of character focus more attention on character assassination than character celebration. And many of the calls for better teaching of character can be truly seen as polite proposals for "keeping youth out of trouble."

But whatever the motives, what is being raised is unquestionably one of the central and most important issues in Western civilization: the relationship between character and the free person, the good life, the just community, and the strong, wise leader.

Leader to Panderer

At the close of the nineteenth century several farsighted thinkers glimpsed the outlines of a dangerous new type of leadership growing out of the vacuum of faith in Western culture. Those who reject the God-man Jesus Christ, as Dostoyevsky warned, would create their own men-gods.

But the era of the Titans—whether giants of evil such as Lenin, Stalin, Hitler, and Mao or giants of good such as

Churchill, Roosevelt, and de Gaulle—shows us only half of the twentieth century's problem of leadership. The last quarter of the century has slipped from Nietzsche's "superman," Dostoyevsky's "exceptional man," and Hegel's incarnation of the "will of history." It has instead given way to mediocre leadership, reinforced by the trends toward the cult of personality and celebrity and toward the confusion over leadership and followership. As contemporary leaders become compulsively attuned to polling and focus groups, leadership becomes codependent on followership and the leader of the people slumps into a popular panderer.

Imagine, some say, that aliens from Mars land on earth and demand, "Take us to your leader." Most earthlings, the response goes, would be at a loss to direct them. Or as Plato warned more than two thousand years ago, the ship of state is in trouble when the crew takes over from the captain and the sailors each believe they have an equal right to steer no matter how untrained they are in navigation.

The complete remedy to this crisis of leadership will resolve many issues and take many forms—among them answers to such questions as, Does leadership really make a difference? And how can we distinguish between a strong leader and a controlling despot, between a leader, a manager, and a power wielder? No remedy for the crisis is complete, however, without resolving the importance and place of character in leadership.

The essential qualities of a great leader, President Eisenhower said, are "vision, integrity, courage, understanding, the power of articulation, and profundity of character." We might add other virtues—decisiveness and a sense of providence, for example. But over against all who would omit character from the list, the Christian would respond with an overwhelming conclusion: Character is essential and central to good leadership.

11

Character's Character

Our three-thousand-year Western conversation about character is now wracked with confusion and uncertainty on all sides. A number of issues require clarification. First, what is character? As traditionally understood, from the Hebrews and Greeks onward, character is the inner form that makes anyone or anything what it is—whether a person, a wine, or a historical period. Thus character is clearly distinct from such concepts as personality, image, reputation, or celebrity. It is the essential "stuff" a person is made of, the inner reality and quality in which thoughts, speech, decision, behavior, and relations are rooted. As such, character determines behavior just as behavior demonstrates character.

Therefore one's character lies deeper than values and far deeper than philosophies, allegiances, memberships, or accomplishments. Just as a nation's constitution expresses its fundamental character and makeup, so a person's character expresses most deeply what constitutes him or her as a unique individual. Character, as rooted in the Greek word for the graphic device depicting a hallmark or distinguishing sign, stamps a person decisively beneath all masks, poses, disguises, and social veneers.

Put differently, the discussion of character is a variation on three recurring motifs—core, consistency, costs.

The theme of "core" is clear from the preceding paragraphs. Character is the "inner form," or core, of a person.

The second theme of "consistency" is an obvious extension of this point. A person's core character is seen best in what he or she reveals consistently rather than in a single statement or a random act. Echoing the Bible and Aristotle, Tocqueville names this consistency "the habits of the heart," while Nietzsche speaks similarly of "a long obedience in the same direction." The notion of consistency pops up in everyday speech when we say that someone acts "in character" or "out of character." For character is more than a collection of occasional behaviors or a set of good intentions; it is, rather, who we are through and through.

The third theme of "cost" is equally evident. The nature of such consistent core character is usually either formed best or revealed most clearly in the crucible of testing. Hence its cost.

Beyond this basic threefold idea, the Western tradition displays many different emphases. The Greeks, for instance, were the first to hold that character was the mark stamped on a coin and therefore the quality stamped on a person. But whereas we moderns think character is what distinguishes a person as a particular individual, the Greeks believed character is a person's share in the qualities of which all humans partake. Their concern was the community not just the individual.

The Hebrews, in contrast, saw such character as essentially moral. "Righteousness" in the Bible is not just a matter of what we do and is certainly not just what we say. Righteousness is a matter of the heart. It is about who we are at the core of our beings—before God. Someone who is well intentioned but who fails to follow through is irresponsible. Someone who behaves well outwardly but who inwardly is resentful, lustful, selfish, or proud is a hypocrite. From such a point of view, character can never simply be inherited. Nor does it just grow like a weed. It has to be formed and cultivated—with help that is higher than human.

This strong traditional understanding of character carries certain implications for leadership. First, character should not be confused with dullness or blandness. Its foundational idea is strength not safety. Second, character can include evil qualities as well as good. Stalin's constitutional mistrust was as much a part of his character as Churchill's indomitable courage was a part of his. Third, in most cases character is already formed beyond hope of major change when people assume the highest positions of leadership. Public relations may obscure what that character really is and may suggest transformations that have not really taken place, but character will always out. For better or worse, character always has consequences.

Where Has All the Character Gone?

The second clarifying question is, Why is the character issue so confusing and uncertain today? Until recently, character has always held a vital place in the self-understanding of Western civilization. From the Hebrew and Christian Scriptures to such great classical thinkers as Plato and Aristotle to the American founders and framers to many of the nineteenth-century European and American statesmen, an influential majority has seen character as fundamental to free, just societies. Strikingly, however, what was once prominent in public discussion and popular understanding has been largely absent for most of the twentieth century.

Some of the principal areas of confusion and uncertainty are worth noting.

1. *Changes in the cultural climate.* Whereas a combination of faith, character, and morality was the rock on which traditional leadership was founded, each of these components has crumbled in the twentieth century. The gap between William Wilberforce, Abraham Lincoln, William Ewart Gladstone, and today's successors needs no underscoring. Expressed differently, it is often said that the United States is a product of three great streams of ideas—the Protestant Reformation, civic republicanism, and Enlightenment liberalism. Whereas the first two have highly regarded the importance of character, the third—more predominant in recent generations—does not. Thus character has become

14

the victim of modern liberalism's double emphasis on secularity and self-interest.

Needless to say, the shift has not been just theoretical. It has been worked out in a thousand practical ways in culture. For example, studies of two popular magazines, *Ladies Home Journal* and *Good Housekeeping*, show that in the period 1890 to 1910 at least a third of the articles were on character. Yet suddenly by 1920 the number had collapsed to 3 percent. Or again, the same trends can be seen, if later, in the heartland of America. Studies of "Middletown, USA" (Muncie, Indiana) show that whereas 54 percent of the people in 1924 said they valued "strict obedience," that number had fallen to 25 percent fifty years later in 1974, when 76 percent said they now valued "independence" and 47 percent "tolerance."

2. *Caught up in controversy.* As changes and crises in traditional beliefs and practices have reinforced a prevailing sense of anxiety, politics has become dominated by cultural issues and culture warring—including "character issues." In many cases talk of "character" acts as a code word for attack ads and a cover for dirty politics. Unquestionably such promotions are disastrous for true character. Revulsion against the hypocrisy of these character crusaders is one reason why many people are becoming more—and not less—lenient about their leaders' character flaws. The beam in the critics' eyes is just too obvious.

3. *Crazy about power.* Power—the ability to carry out one's will despite resistance—has always been essential to leadership. But traditionally power has been held in harmony with two other components: purpose and partnership. Purpose is constitutive of leadership, for without it leaders lead nowhere and belie their name. The modern discomfort with "the vision thing," for instance, is a sign of mediocre leadership. Equally, partnership is crucial to leadership, for without it leaders lead no one. Leaders only

lead when leadership and followership are partners in a wider collective enterprise.

Today, however, these and other vital components of leadership are shouldered aside by the craze for power. Books, seminars, and magazines hawk their offers—the secrets of power in the bedroom, power in the boardroom, power on the playing field, power in the corridors, power in dressing, power in negotiations, power in relationships. "Power lunches," "power handshakes," "power ties," "power plays"—for aficionados of power, the list is endless. We are promised the inside story of what it is, how to get it, and how to keep it. Winning friends and influencing people is only the kindergarten course. At graduate levels, all of life can come under our "control" and be ours to "exploit." "Masters of the Universe" are power wielders par excellence. People are reduced to pawns to be pushed around on a chessboard as life is reduced to power games.

One problem with this view is that it is largely a pose and a pretense. Many of the power tactics sell better than they work. And many of the most powerful people in the world are conscious not of their power but of their powerlessness. The other problem is that the leader as power player has no time or room for character.

4. *Contrived, not real.* Jean Baptiste Colbert, chief financial advisor to Louis XIV, devised a brilliant new strategy to promote France's economic power. "With our taste," he declared, "let us make war on Europe and through fashion conquer the world." French *haute couture* has been legendary ever since. But far more important, Colbert's promotion of style and image has become the currency of modern politicians and leadership.

Style, style, style—if money is the mother's milk of modern politics, style is its lifeblood. Where style and substance were once linked, now style has become an end in itself. The perception is the reality. Identity is a matter of presentation.

16

Style is the art of skillfully packaging illusions as we walk down the corridor of images that make up modern societies. *Vogue* editor Diana Vreeland's motto, "fake it, fake it," is now the First Commandment of the spin doctor and the commercial maker. As Vreeland advises, "Never worry about facts. Project an image to the public." The art of success is to create a world "as you feel it to be, as you wish it to be, as you wish it into being."

Once again the casualty is character.

5. *Closed institutions in an open society*. A fifth source of uncertainty stems from certain institutions in our increasingly open society that, for their own good reasons, decide not to follow the general trends. Strictly speaking, they are not true "closed" institutions—only prisons and certain mental hospitals come close to that. But in seeking to live to a higher standard in a society that they see as having a lower standard or no standard at all, they confront themselves with the challenge of marching to a different drummer.

Churches and synagogues as a whole might be expected to see themselves in this category. Most, however, have actually reached their own cozy accommodation with wider culture. Also, the number of semi-closed institutions is far smaller—including such religious communities as monasteries, convents, and communes.

Beyond a doubt, the most prominent example of the closed institution today is the military. Suddenly leaders of the Western warrior class are being judged publicly not on their military skills and record but on their faithfulness to spouses, their sensitivity to subordinates, and their truthfulness to commanding officers and inquisitive news reporters. Considering the chasm between the military and wider society, the situation is fertile with potential for double standards, hypocrisy, judgmentalism, and injustice.

17

Absurd, say the critics. Only the disappearance of the Cold War and a national obsession with sex could permit the luxury of such preoccupations. But in this case the motive to maintain character and its disciplines has the backing of vital military imperatives. Morals are vital for morale. The choice is therefore cruelly clear. Without the traditional anchors of character in wider society, military leaders must either find alternative sources for nourishing character or it will wither—with obvious national consequences.

6. *The conundrum of perversity.* One last factor in the current crisis of character is that a part of us loves to have it so. It is sobering to look back over history and see how often we are drawn uncannily, sometimes fatefully, to leaders who reach for success beyond conventional or moral channels of accomplishment, to leaders whose character is marked by evil. Alcibiades, Caligula, Attila the Hun, Tamerlane, Lorenzo de' Medici, Napoleon Bonaparte, and Adolf Hitler are only a few of those marked by their insatiable, limitless ambition—a grasping beyond hubris that the Greeks called *pleonexia,* or overweening desire.

What is important is not just that such a figure may cross our paths and interrupt our lives but that so many followers are drawn like moths to a lamp—whether to small-scale leaders such as Jim Jones of the People's Temple or to large-scale ones such as Hitler.

As the Bible teaches and the most profound minds have reflected on in various ways, we are attracted to evil and especially to evil greatness. The one thing prohibited is the one thing desired. So we do not seem dismayed by evil heroes. Indeed, we have a streak of fascination for our fellow creatures with the audacity to transgress. Our age is often described as "permissive." More accurately, it is "transgressive." "It is forbidden to forbid" is the rallying cry and way of life of many of our fellow citizens.

18

Fortunately to this point, such taboo-flouting transgressions are mostly limited to wild academic theorizing, rap-style rage on the streets or the airwaves, and aging sports celebrities—for example, Mike Tyson's self-profession as "the baddest man on the planet" and Dennis Rodman's tiresome tastelessness in *Bad As I Wanna Be*. But the capacity for fascination with such scofflaws and taboo breakers is sobering, and the challenge to strong, good character is plain.

Character Counts

The third clarifying question is, Why does character matter? Currently we are witnessing a resurgent interest in character. The previous dismissal itself is under scrutiny, while initiatives to reintroduce character into education are burgeoning and such volumes as William Bennett's *The Book of Virtues* have become megasellers. "Character counts" is being stressed in a thousand different ways.

To be sure, there are critics. Yet for all the sophisticated disdain of virtue talk, "virtuecrats," and a "new Victorianism," two things bring the topic of character back to the table again and again.

One is the pressure of events. Such problems as crime, mediocrity in schools, dependency on welfare, and indulgence in deficit spending were once seen as essentially rational problems. Viewed in this way they were amenable to purely technical, economic, legislative, or social solutions. The challenge was primarily to analyze the circumstances that created the problem.

But now, as most parents have always known and the eminent political scientist James Q. Wilson has argued, there is a "growing awareness that a variety of public problems can only be understood—and perhaps addressed—if they are seen as arising out of a defect in character formation."

The other reason for bringing the topic back to the table is the vital importance of character to leadership. Far from a cliché or a matter of hollow civic piety, character in leaders is important for two key reasons: Externally, character provides the point of trust that links leaders with followers; internally, character is the part-gyroscope, part-brake that provides the leader's strongest source of bearings and restraint. In many instances the first prompting to do good and the last barrier against doing wrong are the same—character.

Deeper Dimensions

The renewed interest in character needs to rise above current controversies and go further back in history. For example, during two periods of Western history the character issue was given a salience that is directly relevant to our contemporary concerns with the renewal of civilization. The closer period is the late eighteenth century with the First Great Awakening in England and America. It triggered an extraordinary burst of reforms inspired by faith, supremely the abolition of slavery in the British Empire.

William Wilberforce's celebrated journal entry in 1787 is often quoted: "God Almighty has set before me two great objects, the suppression of the Slave Trade and the Reformation of Manners." A moment's thought shows that momentous though the first task was, the second was harder still. Yet what Wilberforce and his generation accomplished in this second area was so influential that historians say their faith was "the rock on which Victorian character was founded." Or as a contemporary historian writes, our present concern for "character and family values" is a pale version of "Victorian virtues," which themselves were rooted in "evangelical faith and character."

The second period deserving closer attention is much further away but is decisive not just for the English-speaking world but all of Western civilization—the writings of Plato in the fourth century B.C.

Plato is not just the world's greatest philosopher but a genius of education. His ideas and examples have made him teacher to the world, his Academy in Athens the school of the world. Following the defeat of Athens by Sparta in 404 B.C., the descent of democracy into demagoguery, and the unjust execution of Socrates in 399 B.C., Plato was challenged to think through a new vision of society. The shining city of the Golden Age of Pericles had become degenerate.

Plato's classic response was *The Republic*, which sets out his vision of the ideal state and of statecraft as soulcraft. At its heart is his new view of education—not the cultivation of skills nor the communication of certain branches of knowledge (such as our "3 Rs"), but the formation of character and the striving to form one's life so as to fulfill the highest ideals of human excellence.

Thus Plato ties the renewal of the state to the development of the individual. The genius of Plato's state is nuclear—it does not lie in its external structures and laws but in its spiritual nucleus, the idea of the Good and the vision of the good life, and the just society built around it. Or what he calls "the state within."

Clearly, for anyone who knows the place of character at such great moments, talk of character is neither a pious cliché nor a luxury topic that is irrelevant in a day of deadlines and bottom lines. Character is an immense challenge personally as well as culturally. In a day when personal crises have become a staple of public life and many public figures are walking scandals waiting to happen, the crisis of character in national leadership touches citizens of all faiths and backgrounds at all levels of society.

This book is made up of a series of readings from the lives or pens of four great leaders from our heritage: George

Washington, William Wilberforce, Abraham Lincoln, and Alexandr Solzhenitsyn. Each section was originally a separate Trinity Forum *Reading* sent out to thousands of leaders across the United States, Canada, and Europe, and now published by demand.

Sterling character is evident in these pages. But there is far more than character here, just as there is far more than teaching. Biography should be a staple in the diet of both disciples and citizens, for great lives do more than teach. They stir, challenge, rebuke, amuse, and inspire at levels of which we are hardly aware. As such, these lives and their reflections show us a leadership to which we can each aspire and a standard by which to hold our present leaders accountable.

George Washington

A Leader for the Multitude

Alonzo L. McDonald

Having had the great honor to serve a president of the United States, a committee of cabinet officers, and numerous captains of industry, I am enormously grateful to what he would have called the "Almighty Ruler of the Universe" that I was not destined to be an aide to George Washington. One could not expect to survive the long and arduous course that carried this remarkable man from his modest role of initial leadership to his final command at the head of a great new nation.

From the perspective of history, we follow Washington's journey with awe and admiration. His path was a most unlikely route to greatness. Although plagued by setbacks, outright failures, and circumstances beyond his control, Washington carried on with a level of courage that raised him above his peers. His persistence, dedication to duty, and impeccable integrity make him a model for aspiring leaders in any age.

A Leader for the Multitude

With the following brief excerpt we honor George Washington and one of his cornerstone principles that should be prized not only in America but throughout the world. His commitment to religious freedom helped to mold what the sophisticated of his day viewed as a motley collection of castoffs and exiled opportunists into a coherent, pluralistic society.

As president, Washington's respect for the individual rights of conscience—not mere toleration, but full recognition of the necessity for personal choice in matters of belief or disbelief—demand our attention again more than six generations later. His fundamental message of religious freedom, "to bigotry no sanction," is an essential doctrine for peace and mutual respect among a diverse people.

Washington would be perplexed by the efforts of some to suppress free expressions of worship and to denigrate religious thought and practices. He would also be saddened by the attempts of many today to advance their own belief system through coercion rather than persuasion and through direct mechanisms of government rather than through appeals to the heart.

Washington was unique among the founders of the United States. His primary education came not from schools and books but by living life in its rawest form, deep in the wilds of nature often with death a nearby companion. He understood how human nature operates during the extremes of life—from fear to joy. This upbringing shaped his later commitments to justice and public policy. Instead of idealistic theories based on historic studies, they were grounded on pragmatic conclusions of how a diverse people could live in harmony.

Washington's journey, at times stumbling and often failing, personified the shaping of a continent and the evolution of new principles of liberty, including religious freedom. His trek began by carving habitable territory out of an inhospitable wilderness; it continued through the precedent-setting process of breaking traditions by launching a new government of the people, by the people, and for the people.

His early experiences were episodes of intensive learning when he was often exposed to mortal dangers. These were the attempts at leadership that the authorities of the day saw marked by failure. For instance, after covering more than five hundred miles through a wilderness where no human had trod before, Washington gave a warning on behalf of the British crown for the French to leave, which they considered laughable. And when as a last choice he was sent back later with a small group of untrained militia to expel the French, he barely escaped with his life, after making many mistakes that led to heavy casualties.

Later as a wilderness aide to General Braddock, Washington had two horses shot out from under him, his jacket filled with bullet holes, and his hat blasted off during a massive ambush. The British general was mortally wounded in the bedlam. He had unfortunately refused to heed his aide's warnings about the different fighting style of the Indians and French Canadians from the massed, drilled formations of the French in Europe. The young aide's role incited negative repercussions in Europe and criticism as the "incompetent Colonials" were blamed for Braddock's foolish defeat. Yet his compatriots viewed the colonial officer differently because he persisted with integrity through impossible odds.

Washington's character dictated his actions. A jealous John Adams acknowledged that the distinguished Virginian had the nervous power, demanding style, and personal bearing of a true leader, but consoled himself that he was uneducated and nonintellectual. Washington, however, epitomized moral wisdom even if he was not the conceptual leader of his age. Others, notably Thomas Jefferson and even James Madison and Alexander Hamilton, were intellectually more profound, articulate, and even more forceful in their writings and speeches. Yet none stood as did Washington at the times of crisis as the leader around whom followers gathered.

The Wilderness Years

Washington's humble origins in a poor and somewhat wayward family gave no hint of instruction in moral values or potential future greatness. His great-grandfather John Washington arrived in the New World as a penniless adventurer who became known as an unscrupulous businessman and the murderer of five Indian ambassadors. After George's great-grandmother died, John married in succession two sisters, one accused of running a brothel and the other reported to be the governor's prostitute.

George's father, Augustine, was described often in the law courts as a restless dealmaker who later denied making his deals. Augustine married twice, having two sons by his first wife and five by his second; George was the oldest of the second group. Augustine died when George was only eleven, making George the de facto substitute father for his younger siblings.

In his early teens George distinguished himself by his gifted riding with the hounds and thus became a favorite of a British aristocratic family who were also distant in-laws. The Fairfaxes permitted the sixteen-year-old to accompany a surveying company to lay out Fairfax claims at the frontier over the Blue Ridge Mountains. Becoming enamored by the wilderness, the young Washington studied surveying during this month-long excursion. A year later he realized he had to make some money and could not aspire to an education abroad, and so he set himself up as a wilderness surveyor. At eighteen he had earned enough to purchase his first parcel of land, 1,459 acres on a tributary of the Shenandoah, and was earning a reputation as an expert in the wilderness.

Shortly afterward family tragedy struck again for George when his much admired, older half brother Lawrence developed a mortal case of tuberculosis. In an attempt to save him, George accompanied Lawrence to Barbados. Again fate intervened and the younger brother was smitten with smallpox. Although Lawrence died, George recovered, acquiring thereby a priceless immunity to the disease that repeatedly swept through the Continental army. In fact, smallpox killed more of his troops than the more powerful British military force.

With his dream of becoming an officer in the British army, young George began the accepted process of visiting Virginia dignitaries to solicit the post as successor to his brother as Adjutant General of the Virginia Militia. Unlike Lawrence, who had served briefly as an American officer with a British expeditionary force to the West Indies, George had no inkling of military knowledge or experience to impart to the frontier militiamen. Even so, with the help of the Fairfax family, George won the appointment and was granted by Virginia the rank of major at age twenty. This began the series of dangerous assignments that ended years later with his charge to protect the western settlers from the Indians.

Washington was shaped by the wilderness like no other president before Andrew Jackson. His formal education, the equivalent of about an elementary-school level, was less than that of Jackson or even Lincoln, both of whom studied law. Washington's formative years were largely spent in the wilderness, first surveying unsettled lands, then searching across hundreds of miles of frozen forests to find the French, and finally for almost five years fighting the Indians.

The endless physical hardships Washington endured tested him in every way. He survived only by sheer strength and indomitable willpower, and in the process shaped his body, mind, and character. He also became hardened to ridicule, failure, and paucity of resources in the wilderness, which prepared him for his indispensable role in the struggle for independence.

Almost by chance Washington was always a leader from his early youth, often chosen as a last resort because others were neither qualified nor willing to accept the risks. Even as a teenager, he looked the part of a natural leader. Tall by the standards of his day (6′2″), erect in posture, and physically strong, he had an impressive appearance that was further enforced by his aggressive, serious demeanor.

Washington's compatriots, recognizing him after his wilderness exploits as an amazing survivor with enormous determination, looked upon him as a hero. His friends remarked at his precocious defiance of death. Myths concerning his divine protection proliferated, augmented in repeated sermons. Admirers recalled when his Indian guide missed hitting him when shooting from near point-blank range; his being spared when every other mounted officer with General Braddock was killed or seriously wounded; his unexpected release by the French from annihilation or drowning at Fort Necessity; and his recovery from falling into an icy river when returning from a wilderness mission, barely climbing back aboard a raft and having his clothes frozen solid around him that wintry night.

With this train of experiences, Washington was also maturing admirably, showing less of his early rashness while gaining a solid reputation for his attention to method, exactness, and fairness. In spite of a short and sometimes violent temper, he was gaining moderation and measured strength through greater self-control.

Although still a highly demanding leader, he sought to follow his "110 Rules of Civility" that he had copied out as a boy and carried with him all through life. He also analyzed and reflected at length on his failures. Instead of inwardly denying his mistakes, he treated each one as a progressive lesson, preparing him better for future challenges.

While enjoying drinking, gambling, and cavorting with other military officers, he was a stern disciplinarian within the army, even being generous with lashes for offenders. At the same time he showed great compassion for civilians, including the loyalists during the standoffs in the Revolution.

A Means to Wealth

The basic values and the character of the man were largely in place when Washington completed his service in the French and Indian War. He had been educated by experience as he studied the diverse natures of the collection of humans he grew to respect. He looked beyond the superficialities of education, wealth, social position, and political feelings to encourage each individual to progress by merit. He also began to appreciate the power of diversity of thought and began to foster that notion of freedom of conscience even in the experts he hired for the development of Mount Vernon.

Washington sustained many disappointments in his personal life. His greatest love, Sally Cary Fairfax, was a neighbor and the wife of a best friend. They enjoyed each other's company enormously, writing and visiting often in his younger years, but the relationship brought a sense of guilt and frustration to Washington. He escaped this traumatic entanglement by marrying the rich widow Martha Dandridge Custis. Slightly older than George, Martha brought to the marriage two young children and a wealthy estate inherited from her first husband. He was enormously grieved that his marriage produced no children and that he had no heir.

On being raised by his new wife's wealth from a common planter to a man of substance, he was awarded the usual offices. He became a justice of the county court, a trustee of Alexandria, an Anglican vestryman, and a grand master in Freemasonry. He also was elected to the House of Burgesses but only bothered to attend when some important local issue was decided. Using his wife's wealth, he greatly expanded the acreage around Mount Vernon and began living the lifestyle of the affluent that he had previously envied. His expenses were soon out of control and "swallowed before I knew where I was, all the money I got by my marriage. Nay more, brought me into debt," a burden he struggled under for the rest of his life.

Unable to be idle without becoming ill, he staked out major holdings for himself in the wilderness. Rather than overseeing this quest from his drawing room, Washington tramped out his claims by foot. Ultimately he gained title to some thirty thousand acres that in later years he sold off when he could find a buyer to cover his debts. Thus he became increasingly land rich and cash poor.

The one virtue Washington hated was personal frugality, believing that a diminished lifestyle would lower his esteem in colonial society. He was right. His assumed wealth was almost as important as his prior military service when he was chosen to become commander in chief of the Continental army. Equating these two, his fellow delegates were overjoyed by his announcement that he would take no salary but only reimbursement for his expenses.

Eight years later he turned in his meticulous accounts, all carefully inscribed in his own hand. The cumulative total was $449,261.51, an enormous sum that would be in the millions in today's currency. His expenses turned out to be about ten times what his salary would have been.

The Call to Serve

Well ensconced in his home environment, Washington assumed his public service was over. He saw the rest of his life being devoted to building a profitable life by amassing cheap land and extending his large-scale farming operations. But in 1774 a call went out for the First Continental Congress to meet in Philadelphia to discuss the increasingly onerous tariffs and trade restrictions placed on the colonies by the Crown. With no effort toward his election, Washington was chosen as the third of seven Virginia delegates, placing well above the fiery Patrick Henry and young Thomas Jefferson, who failed in that election.

Biographers extol Washington's key roles in the First and Second Continental Congresses and particularly in what we call the Constitutional Convention. During the first, he remained largely silent during the deliberations but continued his normal pattern of great conviviality in the substantive discussions in the taverns and dining rooms around the city. During the fifty-three days of the sessions, he dined only seven times in his own lodgings.

Washington left the first congress saddened by the regrettable prospect of war. He had hoped for reconciliation and could not understand the increasingly oppressive British actions. Near the conclusion of the Second Continental Congress he reluctantly accepted the post of commander in chief of the Continental army, questioning his own qualification for the task. He thus became the first and only member of the Continental army at that moment, exposed to a British charge as traitor should this bold move for independence fail.

First in Boston and shortly thereafter in New York, he soon faced vastly superior forces of well-trained troops with overwhelming naval backup. Having some success in Boston by blocking off the British who evacuated their forces from a narrow peninsula, he moved on to New York. There he looked out from Brooklyn Heights as the largest expeditionary force assembled in the eighteenth century disembarked. It consisted of thirty thousand men, ten ships, and twenty frigates.

At that moment the likelihood that a new nation would emerge was hardly imaginable to objective observers. At the outset few dreamed that such a fragile entity could provide a new model for the world not only in human liberty but also in full equality of conscience. On the one side was the

33

most powerful military and political nation on earth. On the other side was a resource-poor, inexperienced collection of individualists scattered across a vast geographic area.

That this idealistic effort succeeded was attributed to divine providence by many, including Washington in his first inaugural address. To others it was a miracle of chance and the ineptitude of the powerful rather than an exercise of strength and genius by the weaker victors. What historians now agree is that this nation would not have been born without the presence and leadership of George Washington.

Being always more of a civilian than a soldier, Washington never saw the Revolution being won on the battlefield. His forces would always be outmanned, outarmed, outtrained, and outfed. Except for a few superb thrusts against an unexpecting enemy, his forces alone could count on winning no great battles. Even later when the British government granted independence, their army and naval forces in New York far outnumbered the men Washington had under his command, and the French army and navy had long disappeared toward home. Washington could mainly hope for victory through the sacrificial determination of the American people.

For some eight years, often by his sheer willpower, presence in the field, and dedication to duty, Washington miraculously maintained an army. In his historical account, Sir Winston Churchill noted that for much of the eight years of the Revolution, Washington's army was incapable of action. "Simply to have kept his army in existence during these years was probably Washington's greatest contribution to the Patriot cause," he said, adding, "No other American leader could have done as much."

The Man Who Would Not Be King

We may scoff today at the thought of an American monarchy, but it was much on the minds of the forebears during the founding years. After Washington's appointment as commanding general, John Adams, who had strongly endorsed him for the post for geographical reasons, wondered if such a powerful individual could resist the traditional historical pattern of declaring himself king.

In a series of dramatic exchanges lasting almost a year, powerful groups gathered in frustration and anger against the inept and impoverished Continental Congress. Their aim was to make Washington king and thereby reshape the future course of the United States. If he were an unwilling participant, they would push him aside and by force "take justice into their own hands." They planned to impose taxes and pay the nation's debts, including its soldiers, many of whom had received nothing for two, four, and even six years of service.

Colonel Lewis Nicola sent Washington a letter in May 1782, urging him to assume the responsibility of king of the United States. The general replied with indignation that "No occurrence in the course of the war has given me more painful sensations than your information of there being such ideas existing in the army."

The following February, this subversive effort gained added momentum as business leaders, distressed over government debt and the powerless Congress, began to encourage military unrest. Alexander Hamilton, then a member of the Congress while still holding the rank of colonel, crafted a letter saying no further possibilities existed for supplying the army. If peace should come, he said, the army intended to take control at bayonet point to satisfy its claims. He also hinted that Washington's own command was in danger due to the sufferings of the army, but that by cooperating with "these men of sense," Washington's "benign control" could allow them to convert a destructive power to good.

Washington puzzled through many agonizing hours in "my predicament as a citizen and a soldier." He could cite no example from history of a people ruling themselves. His country's attempt to establish a representative government was unique and extremely fragile. Anarchy and chaos were prevalent and opposition to a central government with taxing authority was overwhelming. Consequently, Hamilton urged Washington to accept the inevitable.

Later Washington was to thank the Ruler of the Universe—"the Greatest and Best of Beings"—for guiding him "to detest the folly and madness of unbounded ambition." He had made up his mind. Writing that any conspirators would have to move without him, he avowed to "pursue the same steady line of conduct which has governed me hitherto."

But for the moment leaders in the army were gaining strength. They circulated anonymous letters through the ranks, emphasizing the plight of the soldiers and condemning moderation. Uncertain as to whether they faced peace, if Britain so declared it in Europe, or continuing war, the writers vowed not to give up their arms until justice or death.

Ignoring their commander in chief, an illegal call went out for a special meeting of officers. Condemning such "disorderly proceedings," Washington called a meeting of his own for Saturday, March 15, 1783, but hinted that he would not appear personally. The meeting began on a rebellious note with General Gates presiding. The movement was clear; momentum was building toward a military takeover of the civilian government.

A very disappointed, stern-faced group looked up to see their commanding general enter dramatically through a side door. For the first time in his long years of service he saw anger and resentment in their faces instead of affection and friendship. In his prepared speech, Washington pointed out the rashness of their plans, emphasizing that this was their country: "our wives, our children, our farms and other property."

Countering the exhortations to ignore moderate voices, he warned that then "reason is of no use to us. Freedom of speech will be taken away, and, dumb and silent, we may be led, like sheep, to the slaughter." His audience was somewhat perturbed but clearly still aligned against his position.

Continuing, Washington urged patience with "the slowness inherent in deliberative bodies," cautioning them not to "open the flood gates of civil discord and deluge our rising empire with blood." He solicited them to "afford occasion for posterity to say, when speaking of the glorious example you have exhibited to mankind, 'had this day been wanting, the world had never seen the last stage of perfection to which human nature is capable of attaining.'"

His audience was still unmoved. Washington had failed to win their support. He was uncertain what to do next but recalled that he had with him a reassuring letter from a member of Congress. As he took the paper from his pocket, something seemed strangely amiss. Surprisingly the commander seemed confused. He just stared helplessly at the paper; the men leaned forward anxiously.

Slowly Washington pulled from his pocket a pair of spectacles, something only a few of his closest aides had seen before. Then quietly he spoke: "Gentlemen, you will permit me to put on my spectacles, for I have not only grown gray but almost blind in the service of my country."

This simple statement of weakness achieved what none of his reasoned arguments could do. The men wept. The United States was spared a military tyranny. Jefferson later remarked that "the moderation and virtue of a single character probably prevented this Revolution from being closed, as most others have been, by a subversion of that liberty it was intended to establish."

Although again saving his country, he failed to retain the love and high regard he had so long enjoyed. A few weeks later peace was declared, but the officers were still embittered that Washington had thwarted their plans. They canceled a farewell dinner planned in his honor and left for home with no prospect for back pay. Only some twenty officers were with him seven months later when New York was finally turned over to the new, independent nation.

When meeting with them a final time in Fraunces Tavern, their exhausted commander was overcome with emotion. Saying nothing beyond a short, halting toast with tears streaming down his face, he embraced each man and then quietly made his exit for the long trip back to Mount Vernon.

The First President

Washington's duty was far from over. Six years of anarchy had prevailed with little hope that a people could rule themselves. Then a meeting of delegates from twelve colonies persuaded him to attend their gathering to lend credibility and then to preside at what became the Constitutional Convention. He was silent in formal sessions, although some reported he influenced the discussions with eye movements, frowns, smiles, and body language.

> In the after hours, however, Washington continued his pattern of conviviality, urging boldness on his colleagues to prepare proposals that posterity would revere even if they were never approved. Fueled by the brilliant behind-the-scenes work of James Madison, and the earlier thinking of Thomas Jefferson then away in France, a model Constitution was forged to form a new kind of government. Afterward James Monroe evaluated Washington's role in a letter to Jefferson: "Be assured, his influence carried this government."

Without the slightest effort on his part, Washington was unanimously elected the first president of the United States. All of the colonial leaders including Jefferson expected Washington to continue in the historical pattern of serving for life, but he had other plans. He established the priceless precedent in the new nation by the peaceful passing of administrative power to his successor.

As president, George Washington stayed true to his principles and actions. He had worked for a unified nation and was hurt when his two early collaborators became vicious opponents fathering competing parties. With his Neutrality Proclamation he wisely sought to avoid entanglement in the complex international environment in which the new nation was harassed by the British at sea and from the north, threatened from the west by France, and squeezed in the south by Spain. Again he failed to gain united support as the new Federalists favored the British and the founder Republicans catered to France, creating enormous divisions in the country and jeopardizing the young nation's hope for peace and prosperity.

Remaining ever faithful to the new nation's core ideals, Washington became a strong advocate of fairness and equality. Even as an old Indian fighter who had decried the savagery of the frontier struggles, he lamented that the tribes had become helpless dependents of the settlers. He urged they be educated, given equal status as citizens, and encouraged to take up agriculture and trades to become integrated into the society like others of various ethnic, religious, and cultural backgrounds.

Washington increasingly deplored slavery, refusing to split up slave families or to permit sales, thereby losing the normal stream of revenue expected for slaveholders. Acting alone among his Virginia peers, including three later presidents, he decreed that his slaves be freed upon the death of his widow; Martha carried out this instruction the year following his death. Some time later Abigail Adams wrote that Martha Washington, even with her wealth, was having a hard time supporting her very large family of some three hundred former slaves.

Although he avoided using the term *God,* Washington was a committed believer in an almighty being. He devoted a third of his first inaugural address to religious themes and

39

often attributed unexpected successes to providence. While never participating in the Christian rite of communion as his wife Martha did, he remained committed to his personal beliefs as an Anglican-affiliated Deist.

With open-mindedness and a continuing search for truth and fairness, George Washington was a fervent champion of religious freedom for all. In looking over today's scene of controversy concerning the meaning of religious liberty, Washington might conclude that he had failed once again. But undoubtedly he would not accept this failure any more than he did earlier ones. With unrelenting determination, he would challenge us in the modern age to respect deeply the church and all religions as essential institutions for a moral society.

To Bigotry No Sanction

Paul F. Boller Jr.

During the course of a speech delivered in October 1958, on the occasion of the laying of the cornerstone of the Inter-Church Center in New York City, President Eisenhower declared:

> We are politically free people because each of us is free to express his individual faith. As Washington said in 1793, so we can say today: "We have abundant reason to rejoice that in this land the light of truth and reason has triumphed over the power of bigotry and superstition, and that every person may here worship God according to the dictates of his own heart."

Then, expressing his "horror" at the recent bombing of a Jewish synagogue in Atlanta, Georgia, he added: "You can imagine the outrage that would have been expressed by our first president today had he read in the news dispatches of the bombing of a synagogue."

Washington would indeed have been outraged. More than once, in private letters and in public statements, the first president voiced his utter detestation of intolerance, prejudice, and "every species of religious persecution."

His often-expressed wish was, as he told the New Church
Society (Swedenborgian) in Baltimore in an address from
which President Eisenhower quoted, that "bigotry and
superstition" would be overcome by "truth and reason"
in the United States.

And in the fight against bigotry Washington himself
played a role second to none. Both as commander in chief
of the Continental army and as president of the United
States, he always used his immense prestige and influence
to encourage mutual tolerance and good will among American Protestants, Catholics, and Jews, and to create a climate of opinion in which every citizen (as he told the Jewish community in Newport, Rhode Island) "shall sit in
safety under his own vine and fig tree and there shall be
none to make him afraid."

The fact is that Washington was no less firmly committed to religious liberty and freedom of conscience than were
Thomas Jefferson and James Madison. Like Jefferson and
Madison, he looked upon the new nation over whose fortunes he presided as a pluralistic society in which people
with varied religious persuasions and nationality backgrounds learned to live peacefully and rationally together
instead of resorting to force and violence. In his opinion,
what was unique about the United States, in fact, in addition to "cheapness of land," was the existence of "civil and
religious liberty," which "stand perhaps unrivaled by any
civilized nation of earth."

In his General Orders for April 18, 1783, announcing
the cessation of hostilities with Great Britain, he congrat-
ulated his soldiers "of whatever condition they may be,"
for, among other things, having "assisted in protecting the
rights of human nature and establishing an Asylum for the
poor and oppressed of all nations and religions. . . ." The
"bosom of America," he declared a few months later, was
"open to receive . . . the oppressed and persecuted of all

Nations and Religions; whom we shall welcome to a participation of all our rights and privileges."

The following year, when asking Tench Tilghman to secure a carpenter and a bricklayer for his Mount Vernon estate, he remarked: "If they are good workmen, they may be of Asia, Africa, or Europe. They may be Mohometans, Jews or Christians of any Sect, or they may be Atheists."

As he told a Mennonite minister who sought refuge in the United States after the Revolution: "I had always hoped that this land might become a safe and agreeable Asylum to the virtuous and persecuted part of mankind, to whatever nation they might belong." He was, as John Bell pointed out in 1779, "a total stranger to religious prejudices, which have so often excited Christians of one denomination to cut the throats of those of another."

From Differences to Inquiry, from Inquiry to Truth

It is clear that Washington's devotion to religious liberty was not based, like Roger Williams's, upon a profound and passionate conviction that freedom was crucial for the Christian earthly pilgrimage. Washington seems to have had the characteristic unconcern of the eighteenth-century Deist for the forms and creeds of institutional religion. He had, moreover, the strong aversion of the upper-class Deist for sectarian quarrels that threatened to upset the "peace of Society." It is a truism that indifference leads to toleration, and no doubt Washington's Deist indifference to sectarian concerns was an important factor in producing the broad-minded tolerance in matters of religion that he displayed throughout his life.

Still, like most American Deists (and unlike many European Deists), Washington had little or none of the anticlerical spirit. In addition to attending his own church with a fair degree of regularity, he also visited other churches, including the Roman Catholic, on occasion. Moreover, from time to time, like Franklin and Jefferson, he contributed money to the building funds of denominations other than his own.

But it would be wrong to assume that Washington's views were shaped solely by social expediency and theological indifference. Though Washington was not given much to philosophical reflection, he did, on one occasion at least, try to work out a more fundamental basis for his views on liberty.

In a fragmentary passage in his handwriting that he apparently intended to use in his inaugural address or in his first annual message to Congress, Washington asked:

> [Should I] set up my judgment as the standard of perfection? And shall I arrogantly pronounce that whosoever differs from me, must discern the subject through a distorting medium, or be influenced by some nefarious scheme? The mind is so formed in different persons as to contemplate the same objects in different points of view. Hence originates the difference on questions of the greatest import, human and divine.

Without reading too much into this isolated passage, it may be noted that Washington's apparent attempt here to find a basis for liberty in a pluralistic view of human perceptions sounds very much like Jefferson. Differences of opinion, Jefferson always insisted, "like differences of face, are a law of our own nature, and should be viewed with the same tolerance." Furthermore, such differences lead to inquiry and "inquiry to truth."

Freedom, therefore, for Jefferson, was a necessary condition for the moral and intellectual progress of mankind. Washington's musings on the eve of his inauguration are so Jeffersonian in spirit that one cannot help wondering whether his association with Jefferson had something to do with the clear-cut enunciation of his views on religious liberty that he made while he was president.

44

At any rate, it was unquestionably a matter of principle with Washington to treat the "different points of view" of the religious organizations of his day on "questions of the greatest import" with sincere respect, even if he could not share these points of view. As he told Joseph Hopkinson toward the end of his life: "To expect that all men should think alike upon political, more than on Religious, or other subjects, would be to look for a change in the order of nature." And since, as he said elsewhere, important questions are invariably "viewed through different mediums by different men, all that can be expected in such cases is charity [and] mutual forbearance." Charity and mutual forbearance in matters of religion were for Washington prime desiderata in the life of the new nation.

A Revolutionary Aim

During the Revolution Washington had little occasion to make formal pronouncements on the subject of religious freedom. Nevertheless, he made it clear, as commander in chief of the Continental army, that he was firmly opposed to all expressions of religious bigotry among his soldiers. Roman Catholic historians frequently single out the fourteenth item of his instructions to Colonel Benedict Arnold on the eve of the Canadian expedition in the fall of 1775 to show that the American commander was "one of the very few men of the Revolution who had, in 1770, outgrown or overcome all religious prejudices in religious matters." Washington's instructions on September 14 were these:

> As the Contempt of the Religion of a Country by ridiculing any of its Ceremonies or affronting its Ministers or Votaries has ever been deeply resented, you are to be particularly careful to restrain every Officer and Soldier from

45

such Imprudence and Folly and to punish every Instance of it. On the other hand, as far as lays in your power, you are to protect and support the free Exercise of the Religion of the Country and the undisturbed Enjoyment of the rights of Conscience in religious Matters, with your utmost Influence and Authority.

In an accompanying letter to Arnold, Washington added:

I also give it in Charge to you to avoid all Disrespect to or Contempt of the Religion of the Country and its Ceremonies. Prudence, Policy, and a true Christian spirit, will lead us to look with Compassion upon their Errors without insulting them. While we are contending for our own Liberty, we should be very cautious of violating the Rights of Conscience in others, ever considering that God alone is the Judge of the Hearts of Men, and to him only in this Case, they are answerable.

Although Washington's associations, during the Revolution, with the Quakers, Catholics, and Universalists showed that he was sensitive to the rights of conscience and "a total stranger to religious prejudices," only once, as Continental commander, did he single out religious liberty, in a formal public statement, as one of the objectives for which the war was being fought. This was on November 16, 1782, when he was responding to a welcoming address made by the ministers, elders, and deacons of the Reformed Protestant Dutch Church of Kingston, New York, on the occasion of his visit to the town. During the course of their address, the officers of the Kingston church declared that "our Religious Rights" were "partly involved in our Civil," and Washington, in his reply, declared:

Convinced that our Religious Liberties were as essential as our Civil, my endeavours have never been wanting to encourage and promote the one, while I have been contending for the other; and I am highly flattered by finding that my efforts have met the approbation of so respectable a body.

No doubt Washington had assumed all along that "Religious Rights" were involved in civil rights. In an address to the United Dutch Reformed churches of Hackensack and Schalenburg, New Jersey, shortly after the close of the war, he mentioned the "protection of our Civil and Religious Liberties" as one of the achievements of the Revolution. He also told the German Reformed congregation of New York City about the same time that the "establishment of Civil and Religious Liberty was the Motive which induced me to the field."

If, on the whole, he had said little about this during the war, he had much to say publicly and of an explicit nature on the subject after he became president. In each case what he said grew out of some point raised in a formal address of congratulations similar to that delivered to him by the Kingston church.

Shouts of Congratulations

Among these many exchanges of compliments were twenty-two with the major religious bodies of his day. There is, as one would expect, much in the addresses of these groups and in Washington's responses of a ceremonial, platitudinous, and even pompous nature. The addresses were, as the Virginia Baptists put it, largely "shouts of congratulations" upon Washington's elevation to the highest office in the land. They consisted of praise for Washington's services in both war and peace, pledges of loyal support for the new national government, expressions of hope for the flourishing of religion and morality in the new nation, and invocations of divine blessings upon the president.

Washington's replies, for their part, were properly modest as regards himself, expressed gratification at the professions of loyalty to the federal government, and, as regards religion, frequently consisted of little more than paraphrases of what had been said by his congratulators. Nevertheless, there is also much that is valuable in these exchanges for the insight that they give us into Washington's views both on the subject of religious freedom and on the question of the relation between church and state in the young republic.

In thirteen of the twenty-two exchanges there are direct references to religious liberty. Three of the references are largely conventional in nature. When the Synod of the Dutch Reformed Church, for example, pointed out that "just government protects all in their religious rights," Washington said simply that he "readily" agreed with this sentiment.

Similarly, when the Methodists praised Washington's concern for the "preservation of those civil and religious liberties which have been transmitted to us by . . . the glorious revolution," Washington assured them of his "desires to contribute whatever may be in my power towards the preservation of the civil and religious liberties of the American People."

In the same manner, when responding to a statement by John Murray on behalf of the Universalists that "the peculiar doctrine which we hold is . . . friendly to the order and happiness of Society," Washington merely voiced his hope that citizens of every faith would enjoy "the auspicious years of Peace, liberty and free enquiry, with which they are now favored."

More interesting, perhaps, is Washington's response to felicitations from the General Convention of the Protestant Episcopal Church meeting in Philadelphia. When the Episcopalians, during the course of their long letter, expressed pleasure at the "election of a civil Ruler . . . who has happily united a tender regard for other churches with an inviolable attachment to his own," Washington seized the opportunity to remark:

> It affords edifying prospects indeed to see Christians of different denominations dwell together in more charity, and conduct themselves in respect to each other with a more christian-like spirit than ever they have done in any former age, or in any other Nation.

The Baptists of Virginia were far less confident than Washington that a spirit of charity prevailed among the different denominations of the country. They had not forgotten the discrimination they had suffered before the Revolution, and they had serious doubts as to whether the new federal Constitution satisfactorily safeguarded religious liberty for everyone. They took their correspondence with Washington, therefore, with the utmost seriousness.

At a meeting of the General Committee of Baptists in Virginia in March 1788, the question was raised: "Does the new Federal Constitution, which has now lately made its appearance in public, make sufficient provision for the secure enjoyment of religious liberty?" After considerable discussion and a careful reading of the Constitution, the question was put to a vote and decided unanimously in the negative.

A committee, headed by John Leland, was then appointed to prepare an address to Washington on the subject and to secure the cooperation of Baptists in other states in seeking amendments to the Constitution. The address, prepared by Leland, was adopted at the annual meeting of the General Committee at Richmond in May the following year and transmitted to Washington at some undetermined date after the close of the meeting. "When the Constitution first made its appearance in Virginia," the Baptists told Washington in this document,

49

we, as a society, had unusual strugglings of mind; fearing that the *liberty of conscience,* dearer to us than property or life, was not sufficiently secured—Perhaps our jealousies were heightened on account of the usage that we received under the royal government, when Mobs, Bonds, Fines, and Prisons were our frequent attendants.—Convinced on one hand that without an effective national government we should fall into disunion and all the consequent evils; and on the other fearing that we should be accessory to some religious oppression, should any one Society in the Union preponderate over all the rest. But amidst all the inquietudes of mind, our consolation arose from this consideration "The plan must be good for it bears the signature of a tried, trusty friend"—and if religious liberty is rather insecure, "The administration will certainly prevent all oppression for a Washington will preside. . . ."

Should the horrid evils of faction, ambition, war, perfidy, fraud and persecution, for conscience sake, which have been so pestiferous in Asia and Europe, ever approach the borders of our happy nation, may the name and administration of our beloved *President,* like the radiant source of day, drive all those dark clouds from the American hemisphere.

In his reply, Washington praised the Baptists as "firm friends to civil liberty" and as "persevering Promoters of our glorious revolution" and tried to quiet their fears about the Constitution.

If I could have entertained the slightest apprehension that the Constitution framed in the Convention, where I had the honor to preside, might possibly endanger the religious rights of any ecclesiastical Society, certainly I would never have placed my signature to it; and if I could now conceive that the general Government might ever be so administered as to render the liberty of conscience insecure, I beg you will be persuaded that no one would be more zealous than myself to establish effectual barriers against the horrors of spiritual tyranny, and every species of religious persecution—For you, doubtless, remember that I have often expressed my sentiments, that every man, conducting himself as a good citizen, and being accountable to God alone for his religious opinions, ought to be protected in worshipping the Deity according to the dictates of his own conscience.

A Neutral Document

If the Baptists and the Quakers were particularly interested in liberty of conscience under the new Constitution, there were other religionists who deplored the omission of any reference to deity in the document. The Constitution is, in fact, completely secular in nature.

The Constitution-makers were by no means hostile to organized religion, but they were undoubtedly eager to avoid embroiling the new government in religious controversies. The clause prohibiting religious tests for office-holding was adopted, as Luther Martin acknowledged, "by a great majority of the convention and without much debate" and it was certainly welcomed by fervent church-state separationists like the Baptists.

Presbyterians in northern New England, however, were somewhat less enthusiastic about this constitutional aloofness from religion. In October 1789, when Washington was traveling in New England, the ministers and elders of the first Presbytery of the Eastward (composed of Presbyterian churches in northeastern Massachusetts and in New Hampshire) sent him a long welcoming address from Newburyport in which they commented in some detail on the Constitution. They had no objection, they declared, to "the want of *a religious test*, that grand engine of persecution in every tyrant's hand." Moreover, they praised Washington for his toleration in religious matters:

The catholic spirit breathed in all your public acts supports us in the pleasing assurance that no religious establish-

51

ments—no exclusive privileges tending to elevate one denomination of Christians to the depression of the rest, shall ever be ratified by the signature of the *President* during your administration. On the contrary we bless God that your whole deportment bids all denominations confidently to expect to find in you the watchful guardian of their equal liberties.

Nevertheless, they continued, "we should not have been alone in rejoicing to have seen some explicit acknowledgment of the *only true God and Jesus Christ, he hath sent* inserted some where in the *Magna Charta* of our country."

Washington's reply was a clear statement of his views on the relation between church and state under the new Constitution. After thanking the Presbytery for its "affectionate welcome," he declared:

And here, I am persuaded, you will permit me to observe, that the path of true piety is so plain as to require but little political attention. To this consideration we ought to ascribe the absence of any regulation respecting religion from the Magna Charta of our country.

To the guidance of the ministers of the gospel this important object is, perhaps, more properly committed. It will be your care to instruct the ignorant, to reclaim the devious; and in the progress of morality and science, to which our government will give every furtherance, we may expect confidently, the advancement of true religion and the completion of happiness.

Washington's response was tactfully phrased, as were all his responses to addresses of religious organizations, but there is every reason to believe that the policy of "friendly separation" that he enunciated here represented his own considered opinions and those of most of his associates in the Constitutional Convention.

52

An Instrument of Change

Nevertheless, a few days after Washington's inauguration an article appeared on page one of the *Gazette of the United States* (New York), insisting that the foundations of the American republic had been laid by the Protestant religion and that Protestants therefore deserved special consideration under the federal government. In a long letter to the *Gazette* the following month, Father John Carroll vigorously challenged this point of view. "Every friend to the rights of conscience," he declared, "must have felt pain" at this evidence of "religious intolerance." "Perhaps," he continued, the writer

> is one of those who think it consistent with justice to exclude certain citizens from the honors and emoluments of society merely on account of their religious opinions, provided they be not restrained by racks and forfeitures from the exercise of that worship which their consciences approve. If such be his views, in vain then have Americans associated into one great national Union, under the firm persuasion that they were to retain, when associated, every natural right not expressly surrendered.

Pointing out that the "blood of Catholics flowed as freely" as that of "any of their fellow citizens" during the Revolution and that American Catholics had "concurred with perhaps greater unanimity than any other body of men" in the work of the Constitutional Convention, Father Carroll concluded: "The establishment of the American empire was not the work of this or that religion, but arose from the exertion of all her citizens to redress their wrongs, to assert their rights, and lay its foundation on the soundest principles of justice and equal liberty." It is not surprising that American Catholics, like the Virginia Baptists, looked upon the friendly sentiments that Washington expressed to them a few months later in response to their congratulatory address as of major importance in the development of religious toleration in the new nation.

53

The address, signed by John Carroll and presented to Washington on March 15, 1790, by Charles Carroll of Carrollton, Daniel Carroll, Thomas FitzSimons, Dominick Lynch, and Rev. Nicholas Burke of St. Peter's Church in New York City, emphasized the influence that Washington, by his "example as well as by vigilance," had on the "manners of our fellow-citizens." Calling attention to the progress of the United States under Washington's leadership, the address went on to say:

> From these happy events, in which none can feel a warmer interest than ourselves, we derive additional pleasure by recollecting, that you, Sir, have been the principal instrument to effect so rapid a change in our political situation. This prospect of national prosperity is peculiarly pleasing to us on another account; because whilst our country preserves her freedom and independence, we shall have a well founded title to claim from her justice equal rights of citizenship, as the price of our blood spilt under your eyes, and of our common exertions for her defense, under your auspicious conduct, rights rendered more dear to us by the remembrance of former hardships. When we pray for the preservation of them, where they have been granted; and expect the full extension of them from the justice of those States, which still restrict them; when we solicit the protection of Heaven over our common country; we neither omit nor can omit recommending your preservation to the singular care of divine providence.

Washington's reply, it has been noted, was partly addressed to "the great non-Catholic population of the nation." "As mankind become more liberal," Washington said,

> they will be more apt to allow, that all those who conduct themselves as worthy members of the community, are equally entitled to the protection of civil government. I hope ever to see America among the foremost nations in

examples of justice and liberality. And I presume that your fellow-citizens will not forget the patriotic part which you took in the accomplishment of their revolution, and the establishment of their government; or the important assistance which they received from a nation in which the Roman Catholic religion is professed.

He concluded by wishing the Catholics "every temporal and spiritual felicity." Washington's statement, according to Thomas O'Gorman, "is among the classics of the land and one of its most precious heirlooms." Peter Guilday called it "this precious document" and added: "Washington's reply has brought joy to the hearts of all American Catholics since that time; but it was especially to the Catholics of 1790 that the encomium of the first President meant much in the way of patience and encouragement." Later that year Washington's exchange with the Catholics was published in London with the prefatory comment:

> The following address from the Roman Catholics, which was copied from the American Newspapers—whilst it breathes fidelity to the States which protect them, asserts, with decency, the common-rights of mankind; and the answer of the President truly merits that esteem, which his liberal sentiments, mild administration, and prudent justice have obtained him. . . . Is this not a lesson? Britons remain intolerant and inexorable to the claims of sound policy and of nature. . . . Britons, view and blush!

Dispelling the Cloud of Bigotry

Like the Catholics, American Jews were also eager that the rights guaranteed all Americans under the federal Constitution be made a reality for citizens of Jewish faith. There were probably fewer than three thousand Jews in the United States when Washington became president. Dur-

55

ing the colonial period, Jewish settlers in America had at first encountered much of the same kind of discrimination and legal restrictions that they had been accustomed to in Europe for centuries past. Nevertheless, by the time of the American Revolution, as Oscar Handlin has pointed out, they had gradually won civil, political, and religious rights that far exceeded anything that their fellow-religionists in Europe enjoyed, even in Holland.

Like the Catholics, American Jews realized that their future was intimately involved in the achievement of the liberal ideals proclaimed in the Declaration of Independence, and the majority gave their warm support to the Revolutionary cause. They also heartily endorsed the work of the Constitutional Convention and rejoiced especially that religious tests for officeholding (which still existed in most of the thirteen states) were prohibited in the federal Constitution.

There were, at the time of the adoption of the Constitution, six Jewish congregations in the United States: Shearith Israel, the oldest, in New York City; Jeshuat Israel (now Touro Synagogue) in Newport, Rhode Island; Mikveh Israel in Philadelphia; Beth Elohim in Charleston, South Carolina; Mikveh Israel in Savannah, Georgia; and Beth Shalome in Richmond, Virginia.

Early in 1790, Shearith Israel in New York began making plans for a joint address to Washington by all six congregations pledging support to the new federal government and expressing gratitude for "the Enfranchisement which is secured to us *Jews* by the Federal Constitution." But the slowness of communications between the six cities, together with the reluctance of the Newport congregation to participate ("as we are so small in number, it would be treating the Legislature & other large bodies in this State, with a great degree of indelicacy, for us to address the President . . . previous to any of them"), produced so many delays that the Savannah Jews finally decided to go ahead on their own. On May 6, 1790, Levi Sheftall, president of the Savannah congregation, sent a letter to Washington on behalf of Mikveh Israel, which declared in part:

> Your unexampled liberality and extensive philanthropy have dispelled that cloud of bigotry and superstition which has long, as a veil, shaded religion—unrivetted the fetters of enthusiasm—enfranchised us with all the privileges and immunities of free citizens, and initiated us into the grand mass of legislative mechanism.

"I rejoice," Washington replied, in what has been called "gracious and flowing diction,"

> that a spirit of liberality and philanthropy is much more prevalent than it formerly was among the enlightened nations of the earth; and that your brethren will benefit thereby in proportion as it shall become still more extensive. Happily the people of the United States have, in many instances, exhibited examples worthy of imitation—The salutary influence of which will doubtless extend much farther. . . . May the same wonder-working Deity, who long since delivering the Hebrews from their Egyptian oppressors planted them in the promised land . . . still continue to water them with the dews of Heaven and to make the inhabitants of every denomination participate in the temporal and spiritual blessings of that people whose God is Jehovah.

Somewhat annoyed that the Savannah congregation had acted independently ("We do not by any means, conceive ourselves well treated by the Georgians"), Shearith Israel renewed its efforts in June for united action by the other five congregations, explaining, in a circular letter, that "we are led to understand that mode will be less irksome to the president than troubling him to reply to every individual address."

This time Jeshuat Israel in Newport agreed to cooperate ("notwithstanding our reluctance of becoming the primary addressers from this State") and insisted only that Shearith Israel prepare an address in which "your sentiments will be properly express'd & *unequivocally*, relative to the Enfranchisement which is secured to us *Jews* by the Federal Constitution."

Beth Elohim in Charleston also approved joint action and submitted the draft of an address that it had prepared for possible use by Shearith Israel. In this address, which was never utilized, Washington was linked with "Moses, Joshua, Othniel, Gideon, Samuel, David, Maccabeus and other holy men of old, who were raised up by God, for the deliverance of our nation, His people, from their oppression."

By August, however, Shearith Israel, for some unaccountable reason, had still not acted. Learning that Washington was planning a trip to Rhode Island that month and that the state legislature and King David's Lodge of Masons intended to deliver welcoming addresses, Jeshuat Israel, impatient of any further delay, composed what David de Sola Pool has called a "historic address" of its own for presentation to the president while he was in Newport. Jeshuat Israel's exchange with Washington, the most famous of the three exchanges that American Jews had with the president, took place on August 17, 1790. The Newport congregation began by formally welcoming Washington to the city and then declared:

> Deprived as we have hitherto been of the invaluable rights of free citizens, we now . . . behold a Government which to bigotry gives no sanction, to persecution no assistance— but generously affording to All liberty of conscience, and immunities of citizenship—deeming everyone, of whatever nation, tongue, or language equal parts of the great governmental machine. . . . For all the blessings of civil and religious liberty which we enjoy under an equal and

benign administration we desire to send up our thanks to the Ancient of days.

A Champion of Inalienable Rights

In his reply, which he read in person, Washington repeated the "punch line" ("a Government which to bigotry gives no sanction, to persecution no assistance") of the congregation's address, as he was accustomed to do on such occasions, but he also emphasized the important point that religious freedom is something more than mere toleration. "The Citizens of the United States of America," he told the Newport Jews,

> have a right to applaud themselves for having given to Mankind examples of an enlarged and liberal policy, a policy worthy of imitation. All possess alike liberty of conscience and immunities of citizenship. It is now no more that toleration is spoken of, as if it was by the indulgence of one class of people, that another enjoyed the exercise of their inherent natural rights. For happily the Government of the United States, which gives to bigotry no sanction, to persecution no assistance, requires only that they who live under its protection should demean themselves as good citizens, in giving it on all occasions their effectual support. . . . May the children of the Stock of Abraham, who dwell in this land, continue to merit and enjoy the good will of the other inhabitants, while every one shall sit in safety under his own vine and fig tree, and there shall be none to make him afraid.

Washington's statement, which has been called "immortal" and "memorable," naturally delighted the Newport congregation and the Jewish congregations elsewhere in the United States. It has, moreover, justifiably been highly prized by later generations of American Jews. Dr. Morris A.

Gutstein characterized it as one of the "most outstanding expressions on religious liberty and equality in America" and insisted that it "will be quoted by every generation in which religious liberty is cherished." Dr. David de Sola Pool maintained that Washington made a "classic definition of American democracy" when he stressed the primacy of "inherent natural rights" over toleration. Harry Golden said that Washington "articulated his divine destiny" as a champion of "inalienable rights" in his exchange with the Newport Jews. For Harry Simonhoff, Washington's statement "ranks with the best of Hamilton or Jefferson." "Neither philo-Semitic nor anti-Semitic," he adds,

> the "Father of his country" seeks impartially to secure for Jews the rights of human beings. Yet he goes a step further. The probable recollection of Jewish contributions to the war effort causes him to show annoyance at the word toleration when applied to freedom of worship. One cannot but detect compassion, or even anxiety in his letter to the Newport congregation.

Because of the independent action taken by Mikveh Israel and Jeshuat Israel, the New York congregation's plans for a joint address of all six Jewish congregations failed of realization. But late in 1790, when the federal capital was being transferred from New York to Philadelphia, the remaining four congregations succeeded in uniting to present their compliments to Washington shortly after his arrival in the new capital.

Arranged by the Philadelphia congregation, with the concurrence of the congregations in New York, Charleston, and Richmond, the final exchange with Washington took place on December 13, 1790. Matthew Josephson, president of Mikveh Israel, presented the congratulations of the four congregations to Washington in person. The address began by expressing affection for Washington's "character and Person" and praising him for his great services to his country in "the late glorious revolution." It went on:

> But not to your sword alone is our present happiness to be ascribed; That indeed opened the way to the reign of freedom, but never was it perfectly secure, till your hand gave birth to the federal constitution, and you renounced the joys of retirement to seal by your administration in peace, what you had achieved in war.

In his response, Washington again expressed his warm regard for his Jewish fellow-citizens and applauded the fact that the "liberal sentiment towards each other which marks every political and religious denomination of men in this country stands unrivaled in the history of nations."

Washington's replies to the three Jewish addresses have been deeply cherished by American Jews in the nineteenth and twentieth centuries. Jewish historians commonly regard them as "of great historic interest as well as of importance." "For a century and a half," declared Morris W. Schappes during the 1950s, "these declarations have been used to confound the enemy in the ceaseless struggle against those who would subvert American ideals through the propagation of anti-Semitism and other doctrines of bigotry." "These three letters of Washington," according to Lee M. Friedman,

> deserve to rank with the Constitutional interpretations of Chief Justice Marshall and of Alexander Hamilton's *Federalist*. As if issuing an Emancipation Proclamation, Washington rose to the opportunity which the addresses from these Jewish congregations afforded. He gave point to the theory of American democracy which, finally and expressly embodied in the Bill of Rights, struck from the Jews of the United States the shackles of disabilities, survivals of the past in other lands, handicapping them politically and restricting them in the enjoyment of their religion. Too

61

little known to the general public, these letters stand enshrined in a place of honor in American Jewish history.

With the rise of the Nazi terror in the 1930s, Washington's exchange with the Newport synagogue took on renewed significance for American Jews. In August, 1940, the one hundred and fiftieth anniversary of Washington's Newport address was celebrated by Jewish congregations in Newport and in New York. In a series of nationally broadcast speeches delivered for the occasion in the Central Synagogue in New York City, Rabbi Jonah M. Wise contrasted Washington, the man of "truth, faith, and liberty," with the "leering, brutal conquerors of Europe"; Dr. Morris A. Gutstein emphasized Washington's distinction between "two types of liberty: one, mere *Toleration*, another, real *Equality*"; and Dr. David de Sola Pool called attention to Washington's "utter freedom from religious prejudice, and his conviction that in this new America all religions must stand on a footing of equality."

Real Equality, Not Mere Toleration

Two years after his exchange with the American Jewish congregations, Washington had a brief encounter with a little group of Swedenborgians in Maryland. In January 1793, when he was visiting Baltimore, the tiny New Church Society, which had been organized in the city the previous year, "boldly" (as the historian of the movement puts it) presented him with a copy of Emanuel Swedenborg's *The True Christian Religion*, together with an "energetic" address rejoicing that "Priestcraft and Kingcraft, those banes of human felicity, are hiding their diminished heads" and that "equality in State, as well as in Church, proportionately to merit, are considered the true criterion of the majesty of the people."

In what Swedenborgian writers regard as a "rational" and "manly" reply, Washington paid tribute to freedom of religion and then added significantly: "In this enlightened age & in this Land of equal liberty it is our boast, that a man's religious tenets will not forfeit the protection of the Laws, nor deprive him of the right of attaining & holding the highest offices that are known in the United States." It was Washington's final public insistence upon "real *Equality*" rather than "mere *Toleration*" for citizens of every faith in the young republic.

In September 1796, Washington issued his farewell address to the nation. The "wisdom of Providence," he declared, in a passage reminiscent of the notes he had jotted down at the beginning of his presidency, "has ordained that men, on the same subjects, shall not always think alike." Nevertheless, "charity and benevolence when they happen to differ," he continued, "may so far shed their benign influence as to banish those invectives which proceed from illiberal prejudices and jealousies."

A few months later, in responding to the address of the twenty-four Philadelphia clergymen on the occasion of his retirement from office, he expressed his "unspeakable pleasure" at viewing the

> harmony and brotherly love which characterize the Clergy of different denominations, as well in this, as in other parts of the United States; exhibiting to the world a new and interesting spectacle, at once the pride of our country and the surest basis of universal harmony.

The Philadelphia clergymen doubtless realized that Washington himself had played a leading role in producing this "new and interesting spectacle." He had labored hard, while he was president, as well as during the Revolution, to banish "illiberal prejudices and jealousies" in religious matters from the nation and to throw his weight

63

against the "power of bigotry and superstition" in the young republic.

It is of course too much to say, as did the so-called "Shaker Bible," published in 1808, that "the wise and generous Washington" was solely responsible for the achievement of "civil and religious liberty" and the "rights of conscience" in the United States. Still, by the example he set, in word and deed, as Continental commander and as president, Washington unquestionably deserves major credit, along with Jefferson and Madison, for establishing the ideals of religious liberty and freedom of conscience (without which there can be no genuine cultural and intellectual freedom) for Protestants, Catholics, and Jews—and for Deists and freethinkers as well—firmly in the American tradition.

William Wilberforce

A Life of Significance

J. Douglas Holladay

Several times recently I've come across a rather curious exercise: People in a group are asked to put pen to paper and write their own obituaries. To be included in their musings is how they hope to be remembered by family, friends, colleagues, and communities. Projecting forward like this, far from striking a morbid chord, actually provides some needed perspective on what truly matters.

All of us seek to live lives that count. The big question that gnaws at us is: "How can our lives truly make a difference?" As one business executive said to a close friend of mine, "It's easy to make a fortune, but harder to make a difference."

Making a difference, finding true meaning, exercising real significance, contributing decisively to our children, our society, and our generation—whether expressed or not, such aspirations are widespread. As a boy, I remember being stirred by President Kennedy's challenge: "Ask not what your country can do for you, but ask what you can do for your country." We long for lives that count.

For me, that deeply personal desire for meaning and significance is closely tied to a very public question that stalks many discussions and debates in the United States and the West: Once a nation or society shows signs of drift or decline from its original ideals and vision, can that process be reversed? Can a culture genuinely be won back? Or is the attempt forlorn, a futile gesture destined to end in reactionary hardness and failure?

A mere ten years ago the question itself would have sounded absurd. But the mid-eighties' "morning in America," for example, has given way to a widespread sense of deep cultural and social crisis. American conservatives lament the social indicators of "American pathologies" while liberals rue the perils of "cynicism and mistrust" in public life. One widely quoted study in 1996 showed that whereas three out of four Americans trusted the federal government and other institutions thirty years ago, only one in four does so today. A front-page story expressing our dilemma stated it this way: "Cure for Nation's Cynicism Eludes Its Leaders." Similar trends and responses are evident elsewhere too.

But the fashionable pessimism is premature. So too is the failure of nerve of the sophisticated, cynical, and jaded. For at least two great periods in history stand as shining examples of the triumph of truth and reform over pessimism and decline. Complex modern problems may not be soluble by political, legal, and economic means alone. But the precedents in the past show that profound, history-changing restoration of culture is possible through the vision and enterprise of people motivated by a vital faith. Russian poet Boris Pasternak expressed it well: "It is not revolutions and upheavals that clear the road to new and better days but . . . someone's soul, inspired and ablaze."

One precedent, although more remote from our own times, is the saving of Western civilization by the Irish in the sixth century. It was a saving by "the skin of our teeth," as art historian Kenneth Clark said. But the books, learning, scholarship, and culture saved by the tireless Irish missionaries who streamed out across Europe were almost erased by the marauding barbarians after the fall of "invincible Rome."

Another precedent, much closer in terms of time and approach, is the extraordinary story of the lives of a band of men and women led by a little known figure of the English-speaking world: William Wilberforce. An indefatigable reformer and supreme abolisher of Britain's odious slave trade, Wilberforce arguably led the single most effective stand against evil and injustice in all history. Perhaps the life and deeds of this remarkable individual, although of a simpler age, will offer a measure of hope to many resigned to our present situation. As the following splendid essay by John Pollock demonstrates beyond question, William Wilberforce was "a man who changed his times."

Born in 1759 in comfortable circumstances in the port city of Hull, England, young Wilberforce began a political career at age twenty-one with dazzling prospects. As a member of Parliament, the closest friend and confidant of the young Prime Minister William Pitt, and one with access to high society circles, Wilberforce might well have succeeded Pitt as prime minister if (in one historian's words) he had "preferred party to mankind." But by age twenty-five Wilberforce was ablaze with a mission for his life—one that, although daunting in light of the deeply entrenched opposing interests, would change the world.

Wilberforce stated this mission in his diary entry on October 28, 1787, when he was a young twenty-eight-year-old parliamentarian. With the menacing black clouds of the French Revolution rolling up on the horizon and Britain's own social conditions providing cause for grave concern, he wrote simply: "God Almighty has set before me two great objects, the suppression of the Slave Trade and the reformation of manners."

There have been few more audacious statements of a life task in all history. It was a full forty-six years later and only three days before his death on July 26, 1833, when the bill for the abolition of slavery throughout the entire British Empire passed its second reading in the House of Commons. In the process Wilberforce went from being one of the most vilified men in Europe to one of the most loved and revered in the world. As Pollock tells, he was even heralded as "the Washington of humanity."

Historians have detailed the achievements of Wilberforce and his colleagues regarding his "two great objects" as one of the significant turning points in history. England in the early nineteenth century was fueled by the economic benefits derived from slave trading. This heinous practice generated millions of pounds sterling and reached to the fashionable country homes of the landed aristocracy. If the reformers had not succeeded in the task of abolition, Africa would have been transformed into a slave-trading enterprise of monstrous proportions. The combination of the slavery in such nations as the United States and the worldwide slave trade carried on by Britain and other European nations would have created the single greatest moral evil in history. More than any other person, Wilberforce blocked the course of that terrible possibility.

That success concerned only the first of Wilberforce's "two great objects." His success in the second, which is less measurable but perhaps even more daunting, was equally historic. He helped transform the civil and moral climate of his times. No wonder that when Wilberforce died, his own distinctive tradition of faith was described as the single most decisive force in Britain and the rock on which the nineteenth-century English character was formed.

The following essay by John Pollock, a celebrated contemporary biographer, is a slightly expanded version of an acclaimed lecture he delivered in February 1996 at the

National Portrait Gallery in London. He has penned full biographies of William Wilberforce as well as others, including Billy Graham and General Gordon of Khartoum.

John Pollock provides a fascinating introduction to an extraordinary but too little known man, focusing properly on Wilberforce's "two great objects." But as it is understandably impossible to capture the encyclopedic range of Wilberforce's accomplishments in a brief essay, we should stand back and reflect on some of the defining features of Wilberforce's life. Remarkable in themselves, they offer at least seven principles that illuminate what it means to live a life of significance today.

First, Wilberforce's whole life was animated by a deeply held, personal faith in Jesus Christ. Rather than ascribing to lifeless dogma or dull, conventional religious thinking, Wilberforce and his colleagues were motivated by a robust personal belief in a living God who is concerned with individual human lives, justice, and the transformation of societies. At their core was a profound sense of the presence and power of God, giving them vision, courage, and the necessary perspective to choose their issues and stand against the powerful interests aligned against them. Wilberforce, along with his friends, viewed himself as a pilgrim on a mission of mercy, never defining his identity or purposes by the flawed values of his age. This transcendent perspective made him the freest of men and therefore the most threatening force against the status quo.

Second, Wilberforce had a deep sense of calling that grew into the conviction that he was to exercise his spiritual purpose in the realm of his secular responsibility. Too often people of faith draw a dichotomy between the spiritual and the secular. Religious activities are considered a lofty calling while secular involvements are viewed with disdain and believed to have little to do with true spirituality. As Wilberforce came to see, such thinking is flawed at its core and frequently

71

results in a two-tiered religious caste system. Those with spiritual sensitivities are urged to pursue "religious" affairs, such as the ministry, rather than face the tough, complex struggles inherent in the swirl of business or politics.

Fortunately, both Prime Minister Pitt and John Newton, the former slave trader and composer of the well-known hymn "Amazing Grace," strongly urged young Wilberforce to remain in Parliament to pursue his calling. These friends helped Wilberforce appreciate the unique opportunity his position provided to launch a host of important initiatives and reforms. Wilberforce's life forcefully demonstrates that a person of conviction can make a real difference within a secular environment.

Third, Wilberforce was committed to the strategic importance of a band of like-minded friends devoted to working together in chosen ventures. History bears testimony to the influence of individuals combining energies and skills to achieve a shared objective. As the Old Testament states, "One can chase a thousand, two can put to flight ten thousand." In his pursuit of reform, Wilberforce embodied this approach, which enables a small group to achieve extraordinary results. His particular band of associates was tagged "the Saints" by their contemporaries in Parliament—uttered by some with contempt, while by others with deep admiration.

At certain points these friends even resided in adjoining homes in a suburb of London called Clapham Common, functioning as one. In fact, their *esprit de corps* was so evident and contagious that whether geographically together or not, they operated like "a meeting which never adjourned." The achievement of Wilberforce's vision is largely attributable to the value he and his colleagues placed on harnessing their diverse skills while submitting their egos for the greater public good.

Fourth, Wilberforce believed deeply in the power of ideas and moral beliefs to change culture through a campaign of sustained public persuasion. As historians point out, he and his associates actually pioneered many of the familiar modern forms of political organization and lobbying through their campaigns to change the attitudes of their nation. This was no small task, particularly in an age that predated modern media and technology.

For example, in one campaign Wilberforce and his friends presented a petition to Parliament signed by 10 percent of the British people. Or again, Wilberforce persuaded the famous potter Josiah Wedgwood to create a special medallion. At the center of the small plate was a kneeling slave in shackles, and inscribed around the edge was the question: "Am I not a Man and a Brother?" This ceramic tract was designed to provoke a discussion of the moral status and human dignity of the slaves. Wilberforce called such thought-provoking inventions "launchers," as they were designed to launch a most serious discussion concerning an issue of their times.

Public opinion was changed as people became sensitive to the plight not only of slaves but of children and animals as well. Numerous organizations for bettering the lot of such groups had roots with the Clapham friends; they also published books, periodicals, and tracts to win hearts and minds. Wilberforce's own book went into five editions within its first six months of publication and remained a best-seller for forty years.

Fifth, Wilberforce was willing to pay a steep cost for his courageous public stands and was remarkably persistent in pursuing his life task. As one who worked toward ideals that endure, he stands in dramatic contrast to both the "headline grabbers" of our age and those with a "bottom-line" mentality who are concerned only for swift results regardless of long-term consequences.

For forty-seven years Wilberforce labored for what some thought unachievable—the total eradication of slavery from the British empire. Suffering defeat upon defeat, he would not be denied. Only three days before his death in July 1833, Parliament made one of the greatest moral decisions by a legislative body in history, a decision counter to its own economic advantage. Wilberforce and his commitment to enduring virtues had prevailed, despite the cost to his health, reputation, and political ambitions.

Sixth, Wilberforce's labors and faith were grounded in a genuine humanity rather than a blind fanaticism. Throughout his life he evidenced a disarming wit and unassuming modesty, possessing a contagious joy even in the midst of the most serious of personal and professional crises. Marianne Thornton, the daughter of Wilberforce's close colleague, banker Henry Thornton, portrayed the authentic quality of this remarkable man in her remembrance from childhood: "He was as restless and as volatile as a child himself, and during the grave discussions that went on between him and my father and others, he was most thankful to refresh himself by throwing a ball or a bunch of flowers at me, or opening the glass door and going off with me for a race on the lawn 'to warm his feet.'" No dour piety for Mr. Wilberforce.

It was characteristic of Wilberforce that he worked comfortably not only with friends but with those opposed to his views on faith and society. His character remained the same. Without being defensive or sanctimonious, he expressed his beliefs in a natural and straightforward manner. Another description of Wilberforce comes from the Scotsman Sir James MacKintosh, a Radical and freethinker who observed the breadth and charms of this extraordinary person:

> If I were called upon to describe Wilberforce in one word, I should say that he was the most "amusable" man I ever met in my life. Instead of having to think of what subjects will interest him it is perfectly impossible to hit one that does not. I never saw anyone who touched life at so many points and this is the more remarkable in a man who is sup-

posed to live absorbed in the contemplation of a future state. When he was in the House of Commons he seemed to have the freshest mind of any man there. There was all the charm of youth about him.

Wilberforce, while committed to deeply passionate causes, had his identity and contentment anchored elsewhere. So he was a man at peace in the storms of his times, one who integrated every facet of his life and thought within the perspective of his faith. Truly it could be said of him that he lived *sub specie aeternitatis*, in the light of eternity.

Seventh, Wilberforce forged strategic partnerships for the common good irrespective of differences over methods, ideology, or religious beliefs. He attacked evils vigorously but worked with a spirit of respect and tolerance for people of very diverse allegiances. What mattered to him was real change, not rhetorical posturing. In a letter to Speaker Addington, Wilberforce explained his desire "to promote the cordial and vigorous and systematical exertions of all, . . . softening prejudices, healing divisions and striving to substitute a rational and an honest zeal for fundamentals, in place of a hot party spirit." For example, when learning of the plight of a widow of an influential leader with whom Wilberforce and his friends had battled, he and two friends arranged for a lifetime annuity for her comfort and security.

Wilberforce is a powerful example of the old Anglican principle: "In things essential, unity. In things nonessential, diversity. And in all things, charity." Compromise on principle was unthinkable, but compromise on tactics was never a problem. Wilberforce resisted the tendency of narrow partisanship, instead seeking common ground where possible and sharing credit for success with his various allies.

In sum, the life and work of William Wilberforce directly counters the cynical pessimism of our day that an individual is powerless to effect real change. We often think that contemporary problems are simply too complex and overwhelming to address, so we typically respond either by escaping into a private world far from the challenges of the big issues or by exaggerating the role of politics as the engine for social transformation. Both approaches are a dead end.

Wilberforce was born in an age when the privileged classes stood to gain little by reforming their conditions. In fact, they had much to lose. Yet armed with a vital faith, accompanied by a band of committed and gifted colleagues, and inspired by a burning vision to fight evil, Wilberforce decisively influenced this very leadership class and transformed his times. As Pollock emphasizes, "Wilberforce proved that a man can change his times, but that he cannot do it alone."

Are there issues to be tackled in our time? Is there a role today that only a vital faith can play? Are we each prepared to find our part and work with others? Are you conceivably that man or woman in your own sphere of influence on whom God has placed his finger and said, "This is your time, your cause, your calling"?

Tiny in stature but towering in significance, William Wilberforce stands before us as an inspiration and a challenge.

A Man Who Changed His Times

John Pollock

One evening in 1787 a young English M.P. pored over papers by candlelight in his home beside the Houses of Parliament. William Wilberforce had been asked to propose the abolition of the slave trade, although almost all Englishmen thought the Trade necessary, if nasty, and that economic ruin would follow if it stopped. Only very few thought the slave trade wrong, evil.

Wilberforce studied first the state of slaves in the West Indies. He found it bad. Then he looked at the harm to Africa. This disturbed him more. Then he examined the conditions for the wretched men, women, and children as they were shipped—like bales, a black cargo—across the Atlantic. And he was appalled.

The death rate on this "Middle Passage" was dreadful. Every dead slave meant loss to a slave ship's owner, yet hundreds were allowed to die every year at terrible humanitarian cost. Wilberforce hesitated no longer. "So enormous, so dreadful," he told the House of Commons later, "so irremediable did the Trade's wickedness appear that my own mind was completely made up for Abolition. Let the consequences be what they would, I from this time determined that I would never rest until I had effected its abolition."

That was a key moment in British and world history. For a few months later, on Sunday October 28, 1787, he wrote in his journal the words that have become famous: "God Almighty has set before me two great objects, the suppression of the Slave Trade and the Reformation of Manners"—in modern terms, "habits, attitudes, morals." By achieving his first object—after a long battle—he made possible the second.

Let's look at William Wilberforce in his prime. As contemporary accounts make plain, he was an ugly little man with too long a nose. Yet he was a man of great charm. He had a marvelous smile and laughed a lot; he was a man of wit. His voice made you long to hear him more. Underneath lay a deep penitence, but his overriding quality was a sunshine of spirit. His contemporary, the poet Robert Southey, wrote: "There is such a constant hilarity in every look and motion, such a sweetness in all his tones, such a benignity in all his thoughts, words, and actions, that . . . you can feel nothing but love and admiration for a creature of so happy and blessed a nature."

Significantly, he was a stirring speaker with extraordinary debating powers. Prime Minister William Pitt said that he possessed "the greatest natural eloquence of all the men I ever knew." In fact Pitt valued his oratory so much that he once offered to postpone the meeting of Parliament for ten days rather than face the session without him. Such an estimate from a renowned orator in an age of renowned orators that included Edmund Burke and Charles James Fox was widely shared. Wilberforce's speaking, one parliamentary reporter wrote, "was so distinct and melodious that the most hostile ears hangs on it delighted."

William Wilberforce was born in 1759, the same year as his great contemporary, William Pitt the Younger, and a decade before his other eminent contemporaries Napoleon Bonaparte and the Duke of Wellington. His father was a rich merchant of Hull, which made his success in politics the more surprising, as a mercantile origin was despised in that era of aristocrats and landed gentry.

Wilberforce's father died young, and his mother was grateful when her Wimbledon brother-in-law and his childless wife, William and Hannah Wilberforce, had little William to stay for long periods.

These relatives were despised evangelicals, friends of the preacher George Whitefield, a leader in the first Great Awakening, and John Newton, best known today as the author of "Amazing Grace." Newton, an old seadog, ex-naval deserter, ex-lecher, and ex-slave-trader who had been converted slowly in and after a storm at sea, fascinated the boy with his yarns. And Newton showed little William "how sweet the name of Jesus sounds" until his mother, horrified that he was turning "Methodist," took him away.

Later, when Wilberforce had graduated from Cambridge and was a young M.P. and "man about town," Newton said sadly that nothing seemed left of his faith except a more moral outlook than was usual among men of fashion.

Wilberforce had entered the House of Commons as member for Hull at the age of twenty-one. Then, at a crisis in the political fortunes of William Pitt, his great friend and the youngest prime minister in British history, Wilberforce brilliantly won the important seat of Yorkshire—he became one of the two "knights of the Shire" and an immense help to Pitt. In fact it was Yorkshire that made Wilberforce a man of power and significance in politics: Many thought he might one day be prime minister. Thus, in his early twenties, Wilberforce had reached a position of considerable power and eminence. Welcome in the highest circles, privy to cabinet secrets, the closest friend of the prime minister, Wilberforce had a future that was bright with opportunities.

But that winter and spring of 1784–85, aged twenty-five, Wilberforce underwent a deep, long, drawn-out experience of conversion or, rather, a rededication or rediscovery of Christ. He described it as the "great change." Humanly speaking it came about when he invited his former schoolmaster Isaac Milner, now a don at Cambridge, to be his companion on a journey by carriage in the south of France. Wilberforce had not realized that Milner was an evangelical and ridiculed evangelicals mercilessly. But as a result of their conversations and reading, Wilberforce was forced to think. He returned to England in turmoil of soul, deeply conscious of his need for Christ yet loath to abandon his political ambitions or care-free social life. In his distress he turned to John Newton.

Newton led Wilberforce to peace. Equally important, Newton stopped him from giving up politics for the church: "It is hoped and believed that the Lord has raised you up for the good of the nation." But what was to be his new purpose? "The first years I was in Parliament," Wilberforce wrote later, "I did nothing—nothing that is to any purpose. My own distinction was my darling object." But that changed forever as he came to believe that God was calling him to champion the liberty of the oppressed—as a parliamentarian. "My walk," he concluded, "is a public one. My business is in the world; and I must mix in the assemblies of men, or quit the post which Providence seems to have assigned me."

Soon after his conversion Wilberforce was approached with a suggestion that he take up the cause of abolition. He later marked his entry into the battle to a day in May 1787 when, lolling beneath an oak tree, Pitt said to him, "Wilberforce, why don't you give notice of a motion on the subject of the Slave Trade?" But the principal agent in securing Wilberforce was Captain Sir Charles Middleton of the Royal Navy and his artist wife.

Middleton was father-in-law of one of Wilberforce's easy-going Cambridge friends and one of the only two open evangelicals in the House. He was Comptroller of the Navy and was chiefly responsible for its high state of preparation when the French Revolutionary War came. At the end of his life, as Lord Barham, he was first Lord of the Admiralty and the mastermind of the celebrated Trafalgar campaign. As a young man he had won fame in the West Indies; the surgeon on his ship, James Ramsay, had become a rector in St. Kitts until his care and love for the slaves caused the white planters to force him out. Ramsay was now the Middleton's rector in Kent, longing to see the abolition of the slave trade—and of slavery. Both men knew that a trade considered so vital to the interests of the British Empire could be suppressed only by costly, radical reform and parliamentary action.

Abolition of the Slave Trade

Abolition of the slave trade, the first of Wilberforce's "two great objects," was perhaps the greatest moral achievement of the British people, putting right a horrible wrong. Britain two hundred years ago was the world's leading slave-trading nation; uprooting the vile practice threatened the annual trade of hundreds of ships, thousands of sailors, and hundreds of millions of pounds sterling. It took Wilberforce and his colleagues twenty years, and the abolition of slavery itself nearly thirty more.

At first Wilberforce had "no doubt of our success," but his early optimism was tempered by a warning from John Wesley. Written just the day before the great evangelist lapsed into a coma and died, the letter was marked by Wilberforce as "Wesley's last words." "Dear Sir," Wesley wrote, "Unless the divine power has raised you to be as *Athanasius contra mundum* [Athanasius against the world], I see not how you can go through your glorious enterprise in opposing that execrable villainy, which is the scandal of religion, of England, and of human nature. Unless God has raised you up for this very thing, you will be worn out by the opposition of men and devils. But if God be for you who can be against you?"

The fight was indeed costly and long. Twice Wilberforce was waylaid and physically assaulted. Certainly he became the most vilified man in England. Many people denied outright that there were problems with slavery. A group of admirals even claimed that the happiest days of an African's life

81

was when he was shipped away from the barbarities of his home life. And most people, including most members of Parliament, feared change. Such radicalism, critics said, would threaten sacred rights, property, and liberties, not only in the colonies but at home. After all, the horrifying events of the French Revolution were soon on everybody's minds and news of the slave revolts in the West Indies sent shudders down many spines.

To make matters worse, Wilberforce was opposed by some of England's greatest heroes and most powerful forces, including the royal family, most of the cabinet, and powerful vested interests. Admiral Lord Nelson wrote from his flagship, *Victory*, that he would not allow the rights of the plantation owners to be infringed "while I have an arm to fight in their defense or a tongue to launch my voice against the damnable doctrine of Wilberforce and his hypocritical allies."

Wilberforce's initial strategy was to secure abolition by international convention, since obviously the British traders were not going to agree to abolition if other nations simply seized their share of the market. But his early hopes were dashed.

The strain of preparing the massive case led to exhaustion, fever, and a breakdown in Wilberforce's health. Many thought he was dying. "That little fellow," his doctors declared, had "not the stamina to last a fortnight." Pitt had to introduce the first moves, which led to a Privy Council inquiry. The doctors treated Wilberforce with opium, then considered a pure drug with no moral question involved. He never became an addict, but the prescribed doses, for the rest of his life, must have made him more muddled at times and certainly worsened his eyesight.

Recovered, Wilberforce introduced a motion on May 10, 1788, to consider the Privy Council Report (which was a damning indictment of the slave trade). Though feeling unwell, he spoke for three and a half hours and was supported wholeheartedly by Pitt, Burke, and Fox who followed him. His conclusion was stirring:

Sir, the nature and all the circumstances of the Trade are
now laid open to us. We can no longer plead ignorance. We
cannot evade it. We may spurn it. We may kick it out of
the way. But we cannot turn aside so as to avoid seeing it.
For it is brought now so directly before our eyes that this
House must decide and must justify to all the world and to
its own conscience, the rectitude of the grounds of its decision. . . . Let not Parliament be the only body that is insen-
sible to the principles of natural justice. Let us make repa-
ration to Africa, as far as we can, by establishing trade upon
true commercial principles, and we shall soon find the rectitude of our conduct rewarded by the benefits of a regular
and growing commerce.

Swayed by the facts yet worried by their implications, the
House was uneasy. Wilberforce had to make the trade so insuf-
ferably odious that the House would vote for outright abolition. But—and this was possibly a mistake—he ended by pro-
posing twelve resolutions instead of a single, clear-cut
decision, and the Commons turned aside.

As the campaign gathered momentum over the next years,
Wilberforce faced tremendous opposition—from planters,
merchants, ship owners, the royal family, the powerful ports
of Bristol and Liverpool. One of Wilberforce's friends wrote
to him cheerfully, "I shall expect to read of you being car-
bonadoed by West Indian planters, barbecued by African
merchants and eaten by Guinea captains, but do not be
daunted, for—I will write your epitaph!"

To face the onslaught Wilberforce needed all his parliamentary skill, his patience, his sense of humor, his faith
and prayer. "Surely," wrote the slave owners' agent in
Antigua, "the Enthusiastic rage of Mr. Wilberforce and his
friends cannot prevail in a matter of such consequence to
the Colonies and the Mother Country." But others of his
opponents were not so sanguine. The agent for Jamaica
and its slave owners complained that "it is necessary to
watch him as he is blessed with a very sufficient quantity

83

of that Enthusiastic Spirit, which is so far from yielding that it grows more vigorous from blows."

When war broke out with revolutionary France in 1793, Pitt, once hot for abolition, cooled off, putting national interests first. Friends tried to make Wilber—as his friends called him—cool off too, but he replied that while in politics it is sometimes expedient to push and sometimes to slacken, as regards the slave trade, "when the actual commission of guilt is in question, a man who fears God is not at liberty" to stop pushing. He, Wilberforce, would never sacrifice the great cause to political convenience or personal feeling.

In the end it was the war that brought victory at last. Pitt died in 1806. An ingenious discovery by James Stephen, the maritime lawyer, showed that abolition would actually help the war effort. The opposition was outflanked, the waverers won over. The new prime minister, Lord Grenville, himself introduced the abolition bill into the House of Lords.

On February 23, 1807, after twenty years of tireless campaigning by Wilberforce, the House of Commons debated the bill and it was obvious it would pass this time. There was a most dramatic moment when Attorney General Samuel Romilly, in his speech, contrasted Napoleon and Wilberforce retiring to rest that night—Napoleon in pomp and power yet his sleep tormented by the blood he had spilled and Wilberforce returning after the vote to the bosom of his delighted family (actually Mrs. Wilberforce was a most tiresome woman and friends said you wouldn't know the definition of an angel unless you had watched Wilber with his wife), lying down in pure happiness knowing he had "preserved so many millions of his fellow creatures."

Before Romilly could finish, the House rose as one man and turned toward Wilberforce with parliamentary cheers, "Hear Hear! Hear Hear!" Then somebody gave a most unparliamentary "Hurrah!" and the House erupted in hurrahs. Wilberforce was scarcely aware of it. He sat, head bowed, tears streaming down his face. The bill was carried by 283 votes to 16. The odious slave trade was ended.

The Reformation of Manners

When Wilberforce and his great friend Henry Thornton went back after the vote in the small hours of the morning to Wilberforce's house nearby, Wilberforce said gaily, "Well, Henry, what shall we abolish next?" And Thornton, who had no sense of humor, replied gravely, "The lottery, I think." And indeed the lottery was abolished nine years later.

Actually the struggle for the full abolition of slavery had only just begun. But Wilberforce's momentous victory in the abolition of the slave trade gave him unrivaled moral prestige to help forward his second great object—the reformation of manners, his campaign to remake England. This, which in some ways is the harder and less known of the two projects, is also the most interesting and relevant thing about him. It had been going in tandem with his abolition campaign since 1787.

The campaign had arisen from Wilberforce's compassion. Too many men and women were hanged. Venality, drunkenness, and the high crime rate arose from the general decadence, especially the corruption and irreligion of the trendsetters, not in those days pop stars and media moguls but the nobility and landed gentry. The "high civilization" of eighteenth-century England was built on the slave trade, mass poverty, child labor, and political corruption in high places. As one historian wrote, there was little to choose between the morals of the English and French aristocracy in the century before the French Revolution.

Knowing that many aristocrats pretended to be worse than they were because it was fashionable to be loose in morals and skeptical in religion, Wilberforce set out to change the country by changing the moral climate, making goodness fashionable, and restoring respect for the law in all classes. He hit on an ingenious scheme. It is important to realize that the eighteenth century was a hierarchical age, so changing the leaders meant changing society. And in those days the

Crown did not normally prosecute; it was left to the victim or to the local authorities, who often left the big fish alone.

Wilberforce knew that the first proclamation of a new monarch's reign was a ceremonial one on behalf of "the Encouragement of Piety and Virtue and for the preventing of Vice, Profaneness and Immorality." Such proclamations had always been a rather formal and useless exercise except once, in the reign of William and Mary when a society had been formed to promote its aims and had considerable effect for some years: a Society for the Reformation of Manners.

Wilberforce decided to revive the Society. Covering his tracks by "an amiable confusion" he managed to get King George III to reissue his proclamation in June 1787 and then persuade many bishops, dukes, and other notables to join the newly founded "Proclamation Society" and do their best to fulfill its aims. Few realized that the young member from Yorkshire had anything to do with it. Thus he began to give the trendsetters of society a strong social conscience and eagerness to help the poor. The movement caught on.

Interestingly, the campaign was never specifically religious. Wilberforce never tried to enlist the religious or even the professedly moral. Some of the grandees whose support he gained were in fact notoriously dissolute. But Wilberforce believed strongly that the destinies of a nation could best be influenced by deeply committed followers of Christ, and that conversion to Christ was a person's most important political action as well as religious.

But vibrant faith was out of fashion when he started, most of all among the upper classes. John Wesley had hardly touched the nobility and gentry. George Whitefield had done so, but his influence had been limited. As Wilberforce's friend and fellow-reformer Hannah More wrote, "To expect to reform the poor while the opulent are corrupt, is to throw odors on the stream, while the springs are poisoned." Soon, wrote Wilberforce about his own class, "to believe will be deemed the indication of a feeble mind and a contracted understanding."

Wilberforce set out to change that too. He wrote a big book with an immense title, generally contracted to A *Practical View* (of true faith as contrasted with its contemporary imitation). This became a best-seller. He also thought out "launchers," phrases or gambits to use at dinner parties to turn the talk to deeper directions. Perhaps most important of all was his own vibrant personality.

A circle of friends and fellow followers of Christ grew around Wilberforce's informal leadership. It included a royal prince, George III's first cousin the Second Duke of Gloucester whom the Prince Regent hated for his moral stand and nicknamed (unfairly) "Silly Billy." He was a great help as a royal patron. Another friend was Lord Belgrave, later First Marquess of Westminster. I discovered him when I noticed, in a biography, that his son was holding family prayers long before it was fashionable. I tracked down the family papers and then realized that Belgrave was Wilberforce's convert and warm ally. Yet another friend was Josiah Wedgwood, the now internationally famous potter, with whom Wilberforce designed his celebrated "tract": a Wedgwood piece with the profile of a Negro slave at the center and the question inscribed around it, "Am I not a Man and Brother?"

Wilberforce taught too, to the fury of the radicals of the day, that social reform must have a spiritual base, that reformers and educators who reject God will flaw their programs and end by hurting the poor.

There is little doubt that Wilberforce changed the moral outlook of Great Britain, and this at a time when the British Empire was growing and Britain was the world's leading society. The reformation of manners grew into Victorian virtues and Wilberforce touched the world when he made goodness fashionable. Contrast the late eighteenth century (you must allow a broad brush in a brief essay like this) with its loose morals and corrupt public life, with the mid-nineteenth century. Whatever its faults, nineteenth-century British public life became famous for its emphasis on character, morals, and justice and the British business world famous for integrity.

Most of those who ruled India and the colonies had a strong sense of mission, to do good for those they ruled—a far cry from the original colonizers.

The half century after Wilberforce saw a marvelous flowering of Christian faith and a myriad of applications in countless constructive enterprises. In the process the Bible became the best-loved book of the newly literate. Christian attitudes molded the British character, a Christian social conscience attacked abuses left by the more pagan age that coincided with the early Industrial Revolution, and Christian compassion relieved its victims.

William Wilberforce is proof that a man can change his times, though he cannot do it alone. Wilberforce's own philanthropies were legion and he impoverished himself in the process. He was described as "a Prime Minister of a cabinet of philanthropists." But importantly, he allowed no bulkhead between faith and philanthropy. His "good works" included prisons and prisoners of war, hospitals and the poor, reforms in India and around the world as well as in Africa.

It was a contemporary libel, painful to Wilberforce and quite untrue, that he cared for black slaves but nothing for white "wage slaves." The accusation was put about by William Cobbett, the radical journalist, in the hope of preventing emancipation, which he believed would harm the English working class. The libel had little effect on Wilberforce's contemporaries who regarded him as always on the side of the poor, but it was repeated as if proven in a celebrated book of 1917 and was widely accepted for sixty years. You can fault Wilberforce's judgment over this or that issue, but never his concern for human beings in need.

Wilberforce was also a great lover of animals and a founder of the Royal Society for the Prevention of Cruelty to Animals, which led me to a lovely story. His last surviving great-grandson, who was then over a hundred and blind, told me how his father as a small boy was walking with Wilberforce on a hill near Bath when they saw a poor carthorse being cruelly whipped by the carter as he struggled to pull a load of stone up the hill. The little liberator expostulated with the carter who began to swear at him and tell him to mind his own business, and so forth. Suddenly the carter stopped and said, "Are you Mr. Wilberforce? . . . Then I will never beat my horse again!"

But for all Wilberforce's myriad philanthropies—at one stage he was active in sixty-nine different initiatives—the call of the slaves always came first. Full emancipation had always been his ultimate aim. When the planters failed to turn their slaves into a free peasantry as he had hoped once abolition of the slave trade dried up the supply, Wilberforce knew he had to "go to war again." His failure depressed him, and when a friend suggested that the condition of the climbing boys (sent naked up chimneys to clean them) was as bad as that of the slaves, he was "a little scandalized." His reaction showed how much Wilberforce understood the real enormity of slavery. It was not so much the occasions of cruelty but the "habitual immorality and degradation and often grinding suffering of the poor victims of this wicked system." The evil of slavery was the "systematic misery of their situation."

Wilberforce said that in 1827. By then he felt he was too old to finish the task of the complete abolition of slavery. Many of the original abolitionists and his closest friends had died. And Wilberforce, now in his late sixties, was in constant ill-health. His head had fallen forward on his chest. He even wore a steel frame to remedy the condition (this would not have been known by posterity had he not left his spare one behind, "decently clad in a towel," and wrote to his host to send it on!).

In 1821 Wilberforce had brought in Thomas Fowell Buxton to lead the final campaign. Frail though he was, Wilberforce cheered from the sidelines. Just three months before his death he was persuaded to propose a last petition against slavery at Maidstone. "I had never thought to appear in public again," he began, "but it shall never be said that William Wilberforce is silent while the slaves require his help."

Wilberforce was on his deathbed when he heard that the emancipation bill had passed the House of Commons on July 26, 1833. All the slaves in the British Empire were to be freed in one year's time and their masters were to be given £20 million pounds compensation. Wilberforce rejoiced and three days later he died. "It is a singular fact," Buxton wrote later, "that on the very night on which we were successfully engaged in the House of Commons, in passing the clause of the Act of Emancipation—one of the most important clauses ever enacted . . . the spirit of our friend left the world. The day which was the termination of his labours was the termination of his life."

By his last years, Wilberforce's name was said to be the greatest name in the land. An Italian diplomat remarked at an opening of Parliament that "everyone contemplates this little old man, worn with age and head sunk in his shoulders . . . as the Washington of humanity." Historian G. M. Trevelyan described abolition as "one of the turning events in the history of the world." But this is only the beginning of Wilberforce's incalculable legacy—to Britain, the United States, Africa, India—and countless other places, concerns, and people touched by his life and influence.

William Wilberforce lies buried in Westminster Abbey. In a red manuscript book in a country house I found an M.P.'s description of the funeral—two royal dukes, the Lord Chancellor, the Speaker of the House of Commons, and four peers were the pallbearers as his coffin entered the abbey. Behind, most M.P.'s and many peers walked in procession.

The M.P. wrote in his diary that night: "The attendance was very great. The funeral itself with the exception of the choir of the Abbey was perfectly plain. The noblest and most fitting testimony to the estimation of the man."

Abraham Lincoln

The Spiritual Growth
of a Public Man

Alonzo L. McDonald

Six score and ten years ago our forebears pursued on this
continent the most bloody and ferocious war then
fought by humankind. Even today its staggering statistics
fill us with anguish. One out of every five male citizens
between the ages of fifteen and forty fell in that war—one
million battle casualties in only four years. Every family
and community cried in agony.

The dead and dying were strewn across the middle
regions of our country. A total of 529,332 died from a population that numbered only 32 million. This macabre total
exceeded America's dead in World War II by four times.
Two-thirds of these bodies were clad in blue uniforms, but
the fallen ones wearing gray also were so numerous that
the South drowned in blood.

Families were split. Brothers, cousins, and in-laws were
frequently in opposing armies. Over the horizon to the east,
European powers continually threatened to intervene to
their advantage, prospectively crippling the young republic.

In the White House during those desperate years of daily
tragedy was Abraham Lincoln, a modest country lawyer

from Illinois. In today's world, where we decry heroes and reduce potential leaders to our lowest common denominator, this man is recognized as one of our greatest presidents and a leading world statesman over the ages.

It is well that each generation remembers Lincoln—the man—for his character, moral integrity, and evolving faith in God. As we grapple to gain a sense of values in both our own lives and the conduct of our secular and public responsibilities, we should examine the spiritual growth of a public man under conditions of extreme adversity. His ultimate devotion to country, cause, and God merits our admiration. He rose beyond any of our narrow modern labels that divide by sect, region, race, or party.

There are probably more biographies and written studies about Lincoln's life than any other person who lived in his century. Since they number in the thousands, we know exhaustively about his actions, relationships, key decisions, speeches, and published agonies as our president.

But we know less about his spiritual life and sense of beliefs. Historians have difficulty seeing into people's hearts. The fundamental elements of Lincoln's character, however, have become of increasing interest to theologians and scholars. They particularly merit our attention now in a country that demands that its public schools teach nothing to advance any set of morals or values. How would he view the consequences of our culture's growing absence of values?

As we well recall, Abraham Lincoln was a man of modest background, a country lawyer with only one year of formal schooling. His early years were spent clearing virgin forests in the Indiana wilderness for his father's farm. Even on his deathbed, his attendants were amazed at the sinewy strength of the muscles in his arms and upper body.

Abe was a most unlikely president. He had limited experience in government and no administrative background. True, he had served several terms in the Illinois legislature and one term in Congress. He had reluctantly decided against a reelection bid, which he desired very much, because he knew his unpopular stands would lead to his defeat. He lost the Illinois Senate race in 1854 and another to Stephen A. Douglas in 1858, following the famous series of debates that gained national attention.

As a long-shot nominee and compromise candidate for president, Lincoln represented a new party on the ballot that had never occupied the White House. He was elected almost by default, one of four presidential candidates that resulted from a split in the Democratic party and the entry of another new party in the race.

He was clearly a minority president, having received only 40 percent of the popular vote. His presidency had no honeymoon. The press labeled him a disgrace to the nation, suggesting that his short speeches on the train ride to Washington following his election only emphasized his lack of the needed qualities, intelligence, and education to hold such high office.

Because of assassination threats, Lincoln had to slip secretly into Washington ahead of schedule, bypassing several planned visits to eastern cities en route to his inauguration. When installed, this small-town "Westerner" was resented as a country bumpkin even by his cabinet members. Two of these, William Seward from New York and Salmon Chase of Ohio, had been his principal rivals for the nomination, receiving far more votes than Lincoln on the early ballots. Ultimately both were denied the total votes needed for nomination by their adamant political enemies. As Lincoln was largely an unknown in national politics, he had developed few personal animosities among convention delegates that would block his fallback selection.

For his entire forty-nine months in office, Abraham Lincoln was besieged by anguish for the nation, the army under his command, and his own family. The nation was divided and desperate, suffering internally and under constant threat of foreign intervention. The nation's unity, strength, and very existence were continually in doubt.

His army performed poorly. It had everything but leadership. It suffered astronomical casualties, averaging some ten thousand per month for four years. No clear victory was in view until the very end. His 1864 opponent for the presidency was former General George B. McClellan, who favored a negotiated peace even if that meant the breakup of the Union and the continuation of slavery.

Lincoln's reelection for a second term as president was much in doubt. Even after his party's renomination in Baltimore, a splinter opposition convention met in Cleveland. His key cabinet officers and political advisors urged him to step aside since his defeat seemed certain. During the summer of despair prior to the voting, he wrote a private memorandum admitting his little hope for reelection, saying he must aim to complete the war victoriously prior to his successor taking office.

Fortunately for the nation and admirers of democracy throughout the world, two developments largely beyond his control carried him to victory. One was a reversal of fortunes on the battlefield in the weeks before the election. A steady stream of Union victories replaced the string of defeats suffered earlier that year. In addition, most states gave absentee voting rights to Union soldiers, who overwhelmingly supported their commander in chief. Units from Indiana, a state that did not grant absentee ballots, were given a month's leave by General Sherman at the president's request to swing the vote in a marginal state. Although Lincoln won the election, he again was distressed that his opponent took 45 percent of the popular vote and was humiliated that his home county of Sangamon in Illinois voted against him.

Within his family, Lincoln's own household was split like the nation. His wife's oldest brother and the husband of a half sister went into the Union army. Joining up with the Confederates were Mary Todd Lincoln's youngest brother, three half brothers, and the husbands of three half sisters.

Alec, Mary's little brother, was killed in August of 1863 in fighting near Baton Rouge. Ben Hardin Helm, a brother-in-law and Confederate general, was killed in the Battle of Chickamauga in September 1863. Helm's widow, Mary's much loved little sister, Emily, was invited into the White House to be with her sister. Both sisters needed much consolation as the Lincolns had lost their dear son, Willie, the year before at the age of eleven. They had earlier buried another son, Eddie, who had died at age four. Thus even at his family dinner table, Lincoln could not escape the tragedy and death that engulfed the nation in conflict. Emily's extended presence and Mary's relations fighting for the South fueled rumors that a Confederate spy was even harbored in the executive mansion.

What could sustain a man who bore such a heavy burden of responsibility during this period of intense trial? How could he think clearly and retain his convictions against a wave of negativism, continual criticism, personal and public tragedy, and unceasing barrages of ridicule and hatred? Yet reports from his cabinet members and other intimates suggest that Lincoln became calm in his demeanor, confident in his actions, and increasingly clear minded and committed to his cause.

In the world's eyes, Abraham Lincoln was not a religious man. He never joined a church. He ascribed to no denomination or religious creed. He only rented a pew, attending church services regularly with his wife who was a member. He sat out of sight in a side chamber in her Washington church, reverently kneeling in unison with the congregation. But far more important, Lincoln was a praying man and a Bible reader, increasingly so as the dreary days of death, defeat, and pessimism encircled him.

Looking beyond the limited perspectives of worldly institutions and archivists, theologians now realize that Lincoln became our most spiritual president. Like most of us, he matured best in sorrow and found profound meaning in deep anguish. In almost complete despair, he increasingly turned to God, praying daily—but not publicly. He was concerned only with the substance and meaning of prayer. As he reiterated in several intimate conversations, his chief form of prayer was to seek and follow the will of God, not to change that infinite will.

Lincoln had great familiarity with the Bible. He learned to read it as a boy since it was the only book in the Indiana wilderness school he briefly attended. He told of the children lining up to read one after another from that Bible. Abe was ten before his father could afford a Bible for their own home, their first book. He read from it almost nightly.

His wide biblical knowledge was repeatedly employed during his White House years. He adroitly—at times humorously—referred to or countered religious or political arguments with biblical passages. He particularly liked the psalms. "They are the best," he confided to a friend. "I find something in them for every day of the year." Lincoln even framed his remarks at Gettysburg in the widely familiar language patterns of his King James Version of the Bible.

In the depths of despair in 1862, after repeated losses by the Union army, Lincoln composed "Meditations on the Divine Will," later found by his secretary in his papers. He wrote this document when he feared the war would be lost. After he privately committed this spiritual thought process to writing, the whole tone and content of his speeches changed. As historians have noted, "A gigantic figure had emerged."

Lincoln surmised that the Civil War was part of God's wrath for our nation's sins and slavery. He concluded that the Almighty had placed him in the presidency as a humble instrument of God's will. He confided to his secretary that "I have been driven many times upon my knees by the overwhelming conviction that I had nowhere else to go." As many of us have seen, his statue, with him on bended knee, presently graces the National Cathedral in Washington.

Theologians have increasingly lauded Lincoln's spiritual views and marveled over his evolving closer relationship with his Creator. Such noted theologians as Reinhold Niebuhr have rated his pragmatic theology as more enlightened than that of his contemporary church leaders.

More important than his statements, Lincoln's spiritual commitment was clearly reflected by his example. He was never self-righteous and was ever humble, acknowledging his spiritual doubts and making himself vulnerable and open to God's will.

The president was increasingly decisive as his spiritual commitment became the source of his strength. With the Emancipation Proclamation, he made a one-man decision that satisfied neither side in the slavery controversy at the time. Without asking their advice, he announced his decision to his cabinet, revealing that this act was to carry out "a solemn vow before God."

Several cabinet members argued that such a move was politically damaging, might undermine his slim support in Congress, and could put the opposition in the majority at the upcoming midterm elections. He accepted only the advice of Secretary of State Seward that he delay his announcement until after a Union victory. Five days after the Battle of Antietam on September 17, 1862, during which the Union army finally prevailed, Lincoln made his preliminary announcement. It was followed by the actual Proclamation, effective January 1, 1863.

As both a lawyer and a politician, he was concerned to make sure his actions were not only constitutionally and legally correct but could not be readily overturned or rejected. He also wished to avoid the requirement for a prior political consensus either within his cabinet or by Congress, since he feared the proposition would lose in both bodies. He therefore ingeniously implemented the Emancipation Proclamation as a personal order of the commander in chief, covering occupied and Secessionists' territories only. His order had no impact on slavery in the border states or in any other Union territories, although he earnestly hoped they would move to free slaves within their borders.

Although the Emancipation Proclamation actually freed not a single slave, it changed the whole course of American history by establishing a moral direction. That courageous, carefully considered act inspired the North, further disheartened the South, and brought the Union new support and greater assurance of neutrality from foreign powers. This dramatic act of one man's courage and conviction opened the way for the Constitution's Thirteenth Amendment to be passed by the Congress shortly before Lincoln's death, thereafter freeing all slaves within the jurisdiction of the United States.

Lincoln was a master in understanding the paradox of choosing between "the lesser of two evils." He recognized well that frequently there is no feasible, absolutely "right" answer. Therefore he considered the responsibility of the leader to move firmly and consistently along paths that may not have been ideal in themselves, just as with the Emancipation Proclamation, but which represented pragmatic steps advancing the lesser of two evils. These may have been modest actions when viewed in isolation, but were positive steps that could well open the door for greater progress.

Lincoln was also a man who determined his central commitment—to preserve the Union. This was his priority over all others, even before freedom for the slaves. He fully realized that without preserving the Union there was no hope to abolish the widespread evils inherent in slavery or prevent them from spreading westward.

His vision was far greater than even the unity of the United States as a single nation. During his time in the White House, he gradually sensed that this country was the first great symbol of democracy with a set of values and aspirations for its people—even though far short in practice of its ideals—that could serve as humankind's best example and hope for the future. He therefore considered the preservation of the Union essential to demonstrate to the world that a democracy could live and retain cohesion. Democracy could survive even its own internal explosions. It could prevail as a viable form of government and continue down the gradual path of progress for the ultimate good of all.

Abraham Lincoln would not have understood our present secular attitude in which even the mention of God's name is shunned except in profanity. In contrast, in his forty-nine months as president, Lincoln issued nine separate calls for national days of public penance, fasting, prayer, and thanksgiving. This total exceeds that of any other president before or since. He was preparing his tenth such call when assassinated.

In reflecting on Lincoln's values and religious beliefs, we should recall that he inaugurated our national Thanksgiving Day as an annual holiday on the last Thursday of November, 1863. That event had been held only sporadically before on plantations in Massachusetts and Virginia. He would certainly be amazed to learn that today some of our public school teachers refer to this day as one of thanksgiving to the Indians for their assistance to early settlers. There is no mention of thanksgiving to God, which was its original purpose in the colonies and in Lincoln's tradition-setting proclamation.

It was also during Lincoln's presidency that the phrase "One Nation, Under God" was first articulated. He added this expression extemporaneously to his written address at Gettysburg, which was then picked up by the newspapers in their reporting of the famous speech. The phrase "One Nation, Under God" was later included in our salute to the flag. Also the phrase "In God We Trust," which adorns our coins, was first used during Lincoln's administration.

Lincoln's conviction that God's will would prevail, and that his own role was simply to be a willing instrument of God's will, became increasingly evident in his public utterances. In his Second Inaugural Address, delivered only five weeks before his assassination, Lincoln climaxed his declarations as a man of faith. It was a short speech, written only by himself, in contrast to his initial Inaugural Address, which was five times longer with large sections written by Seward. Yet, even in its brevity, this Second Inaugural included fourteen references to God, many scriptural allusions, and four direct biblical quotations.

That great speech, which is carved on the marble walls of the Lincoln Memorial in Washington, was universally praised in America and abroad. Even the *London Spectator,* a longtime Lincoln critic, called it "the noblest political document known to history." In it was his central theme summarizing his belief that "the Almighty has His own purposes."

Reflecting his spiritual growth, Abraham Lincoln was generous and kind, with no sense of hatred or revenge in his references to the Confederate insurgents in the closing days of the war. As he so clearly stated, "With malice toward none, with charity for all; with firmness in the right, as God gives us to see the right, let us strive on to finish the work we are in; to bind up the Nation's wounds."

It was under his direct instructions that General Grant was generous in both the terms and conditions given the

Confederate officers and men who surrendered with General Robert E. Lee just six days before Lincoln's death. When meeting with his cabinet on the Friday he was shot, Lincoln again emphasized that no malice should be held and that the wayward brothers should be brought back into the fold to assume their full responsibilities as citizens of a united nation. With Lincoln's death, that was not to be.

That work of healing in our nation is not yet finished. One needs only to consider our wounds, divisions, internal violence, and pervasive self-centeredness. Instead of emphasizing our common aims and desperate needs for peaceful cohesion, we celebrate an increasing number of divisions in our society by over-emphasizing multicultural differences.

The growing vacuum in moral values among our people is evident everywhere. Just as in Lincoln's day, it is timely that we again turn to God in humble prayer and ask in Lincoln's words, that "this nation, *under God*, shall have a new birth of freedom; and that government of the people, by the people and for the people, shall not perish from the earth."

Although an uncomfortable thought for many in this modern age of scientific and technological achievement, the example of prayer and the overriding spiritual conclusions of Abraham Lincoln merit our current attention and thoughtful reflection regardless of our beliefs or nonbeliefs: "The Almighty has His own purposes." This may ring true for us both as individuals and as a nation.

Theologian
of American Anguish

Elton Trueblood

Only a few persons in human history have so towered above their contemporaries that they are universally recognized as belonging to the ages. One such person was born in a one-room cabin near Hodgenville, Kentucky, on February 12, 1809, and died, as the victim of an assassin's bullet, on April 15, 1865. The magnitude of this man's accomplishment has attracted so much attention that thousands of books and even entire libraries have been devoted to an effort to understand the mystery of his greatness. Though Abraham Lincoln is not easy to understand and though answers are never simple, he is more understandable today than ever before. The new possibility of understanding arises, in part, from the similarity between our time and his. Again there is in the American spirit deep division and consequent anguish. The chance that his thinking may illuminate our own is a good reason for its reexamination.

The Public Crucible

Lincoln's greatness was revealed in its fullness only at the end of the story, after months of turmoil not merely in the nation but in his own mind. While he is remembered primarily for his difficult political decisions that kept the Union intact, the more we study them the more we realize that all of them were reached at a level far deeper than that of politics. Underlying all particular decisions was a moral revulsion against human slavery, a mystical sense of the importance of the Union, and an abiding conviction that the divine order could be ascertained and followed. One of the most revealing items, as we search for the secret of Lincoln's achievement, is his letter to the Quaker woman Eliza Gurney, written September 4, 1864. In this message, addressed to a private person, Lincoln expressed succinctly something of the anguish that he sensed in others and that reflected his own inner turmoil. "Your people," he wrote, "have had, and are having, a very great trial. On principle, and faith, opposed to both war and oppression, they can only practically oppose oppression by war." The difficulty was not that of following a moral principle at personal cost; the difficulty was that of knowing what to do when there is more than one principle, and when the principles clash.

His Spiritual Foundation

Increasingly, it is clear that the major key to Lincoln's greatness is his spiritual depth. His Second Inaugural, which has been widely acclaimed as the noblest state paper of the nineteenth century, is also recognized by those who study it carefully as a theological classic. The political sagacity rested in large measure upon a spiritual foundation.

To some people it seems strange to refer to Abraham Lincoln as a theologian. After all, his schooling was negligible; he was never a member of a church; certainly he did not think of himself as a professional in religious thinking. Far from being always confident, he passed through periods of uncertainty and doubt. In October 1863, less than eighteen months before his death, he wrote: "I have often wished that I was a more devout man than I am." A major element in Lincoln's greatness was the way in which he could hold a strong moral position without the usual accompaniment of self-righteousness.

What is perhaps most strange of all is the magnitude of the difference that Lincoln was able to make in the religious life of the nation. It has been customary to speak of Lincoln as the "savior" of the Union, but we are nearer to the truth when we speak of him as its creator, since the Union became much more genuine as a result of his efforts than it had ever been before. Previous to Lincoln, the Union was still largely a dream, but he changed the entire picture by the character of his own commitment. There were many threats of secession before 1861, some coming even from New England, but after Lincoln such threats have not been seriously repeated. "The Civil War," said Dean Sperry, "has proved to be not so much the fortress where the Union was preserved as the fiery furnace where men were smelted together into one political stuff."

The change in the national capital, after Lincoln, was striking. The nation henceforth possessed two striking new symbols, the dome on the hill and the memory of a man who cared supremely about the Union. What emerged was a new mystique, which has not been entirely lost in the subsequent years. Part of the mystique has arisen from the way in which Lincoln refused to be satisfied with simplistic answers. He had, in fact, as little sympathy with the instant abolitionists as he had with the apologists for slavery. Deeply convinced of the reality of the divine will, he had no patience at all with any who were perfectly sure that they knew the details of the divine will. His faith in the service that America, under God, might give to the world can be understood only when it is placed in the setting of the religious experience that came to dominate his nights and days.

A Spiritual Pilgrimage

The profundity of Lincoln's religious thinking that emerged during his days in the White House was not only new to the nation; it was also new to the man himself. One of the important features of Lincoln's theology is the fact that it was a *development*. The man had an amazing ability to grow. Lincoln, more than most persons, changed radically with the years and particularly with the heavy demands that events made on him. He changed even in literary style. The most loyal reader of Lincoln's addresses is bound to admit that some of his early speaking and writing style was commonplace and pedestrian. There is very little in the early utterances to prepare us for the brilliance of the Message to Congress (December 1, 1862), the magnificent simplicity of the Gettysburg Address (November 19, 1863), and the profundity of the Second Inaugural (March 4, 1865). But before all of these masterpieces came the unforgettable "Meditation on the Divine Will," which has such a haunting quality that we can with difficulty put it down. As John Hay said, "It was not written to be seen of men," but it will be honored as long as men know what it is to suffer and to face difficult moral decisions.

The will of God prevails. In great contests each party claims to act in accordance with the will of God. Both may be, and one must be wrong. God can not be *for*, and *against*, the same thing at the same time. In the present civil war it is quite possible that God's purpose is something different from the purpose of either party—and yet the human instrumentalities, working just as they do, are of the best adaptation to effect His purpose. I am almost ready to say this is probably true—that God wills this contest, and wills that it shall not end yet. By His mere quiet power, on the minds of the now contestants, He could have either *saved* or *destroyed* the Union without a human contest. Yet the contest began. And having begun He could give the final victory to either side any day. Yet the contest proceeds.

The document is undated, but appears to have been written in September 1862, after the deep disappointment of the Second Battle of Bull Run. It provides one of the best exhibitions of the theology of anguish. Attorney General Bates reported that early in September 1862, Lincoln seemed "wrung by the bitterest anguish." The president, for some reason, left the meditation on his desk, where John Hay found it and copied it. As Carl Sandburg has said, the sad man was "musing on the role of Providence in the dust of events."

The spiritual level of the meditation of 1862 is radically different from anything exhibited in the writings of the prairie years. Indeed, it has been possible, by referring to early statements independent of later developments, to represent Lincoln as an unbeliever. But, by recognizing growth, we can save Lincoln from both his uncritical admirers and his uncritical detractors. There were a few hints of theological depth even in the years before the crucial autumn of 1862, but they are the exception rather than the rule. Lincoln's was the kind of mind that did not reach its true magnitude except in experiences of sorrow and of strain.

Thus, in the emotional parting at the Springfield railroad station on February 11, 1861, Lincoln rose at least temporarily to a great height. "I now leave," he said,

> not knowing when, or whether ever, I may return, with a task before me greater than that which rested upon Washington. Without the assistance of that Divine Being, who ever attended him, I cannot succeed. With that assistance I cannot fail. Trusting in Him, who can go with me, and remain with you and be everywhere for good, let us confidently hope that all will yet be well. To His care commending you, as I hope in your prayers you will commend me, I bid you an affectionate farewell.

109

On the long journey to Washington, with numerous stops over a period of eleven days, the president-elect made many brief addresses, most of which are not really notable. An exception is provided in the unexpected phrase, depicting Americans as God's "almost chosen people," which was uttered at Trenton on February 21, 1861. Here the idea of a national vocation received one of its first clear expressions. The sentence that includes the surprise twist is: "I am exceedingly anxious that this Union, the Constitution, and the liberties of the people shall be perpetuated in accordance with the original idea for which that struggle was made, and I shall be most happy indeed if I shall be an humble instrument in the hands of the Almighty, and of this, his almost chosen people, for perpetuating the object of that great struggle."

The struggle here mentioned was, in part, that of the American Revolution, but it was also something more. It was this extra that continued to haunt Lincoln as president until his last tragic days. The vision that was slowly becoming clarified was, he said, "something even more than National Independence; that something that held out a great promise to all the people of the world to all times to come." The vision, which transcended all mere nationalism, was becoming highly prophetic. Twenty months later, in the Annual Message to Congress of December 1, 1862, the dream was given an even sharper expression when the man born in a Kentucky cabin wrote, "We shall nobly save, or meanly lose, the last best hope of earth."

Very few expected the kind of greatness that emerged in Lincoln's final phase. Because we have known the climactic utterances all our lives, many of us being able to repeat every word of the Gettysburg Address, it is difficult to understand the ridicule that Lincoln was forced to endure as he entered into the highest office. In an editorial the Baltimore *Sun* said, "Had we any respect for Mr. Lincoln, official or personal, as a man, or as President-elect of the United States, his career and speeches on his way to the seat of government would have cruelly impaired it." To make their harsh judgment even more clear the editors continued, "We do not believe the Presidency can ever be more degraded by any of his successors, than it has been by him, even before his inauguration."

An Embattled Middle Ground

Increasingly, whether in religion or in politics, Lincoln occupied an embattled middle ground. As in religion he had to fight on two fronts, so he fought in the political arena. His position was naturally criticized as much by the militant abolitionists as it was by the militant proponents of the extension of slavery. Even to this day there are writers, including theological ones, who claim to be shocked when they discover that Lincoln did not affirm the factual equality of the races. He did not claim this because it was not the point at issue. The question, he said over and over, is not what a man's particular abilities may be, but what his rights are as a human being made in God's image. He listened to the arguments of the pro-slavery party, especially the argument that slavery was good for the slave. The peculiarity of slavery, he said, consists of the fact "that it is the only good thing which no man ever seeks the good of, *for himself.*"

More and more Lincoln dealt with the problem of human slavery, not merely on the political level, but upon a far deeper one. Thus, at New Haven, Connecticut, on March 6, 1860, he said, "We think Slavery a great moral wrong, and while we do not claim the right to touch it where it exists, we wish to treat it as a wrong in the Territories, where our votes will reach it. We think that a respect for ourselves, a regard for future generations and for the God that made us, require that we put down this wrong where our votes will properly reach it." This position did not satisfy the abolitionists any more than it satisfied the slave party, but Lincoln followed it because he was keenly aware of the limitations that fidelity to the Constitution imposed. As an instrument of the divine will he was devoted to the possible! This decision required that emphasis be placed upon *extension*.

This is why, after he was elected, Lincoln wrote to Alexander H. Stephens as follows: "You think slavery is *right* and ought to be extended; while we think it is *wrong* and ought to be restricted. That I suppose is the rub. It certainly is the only substantial difference between us." Two and a half months later, these same words were employed in Lincoln's First Inaugural Address, delivered March 4, 1861. Much as he was convinced that slavery was wrong, he rejected the argument that it should therefore be attacked by force where it was legally established. Emancipation was right on principle, but peaceful union was also right on principle.

A Process of Crystallization

There are many mysteries about the life of Abraham Lincoln, but no mystery is greater than that of the radical change that occurred in his public work after he had entered the White House. The change, which is evident in many ways, is most obvious in the realm of public discourse. The style of his last great utterances, beginning with the "Meditation on the Divine Will" in September 1862, is of a totally different character from anything that Lincoln produced in previous years. The First Inaugural had a certain grandeur, but the sentences most often quoted, at the end, were partly the work of Seward. It was only after he took office, and after the terrible sense of division in his beloved country had fully come upon him, that totally new and unsuspected powers began to be made manifest.

During his first year as president, Lincoln was faced with public criticism of a bitterness that is hard to believe. All men in public life are forced to bear abuse, but few have faced as much as Lincoln faced day after day. The writers in the newspapers could sound smart because they did not have the responsibilities of decision, and they could sound bold by enunciating extreme positions that they were not required to implement. Lincoln, by contrast, in order to maintain integrity had to reject extremes because he was sworn to be faithful to the welfare of the entire nation.

The early weeks of 1862 were dark indeed, partly because of the death of Willie, who was undoubtedly the president's favorite child. Willie died in the White House on February 20, 1862, at the age of eleven. In some ways the sorrow was like that produced by the death of Eddie twelve years earlier, but the new sadness was enhanced by the constant sense of the national tragedy that had not been present when the first death occurred in 1850. Lincoln's melancholy after Willie died was so deep that it seemed impossible to believe that the old buoyancy would ever return. The depression seemed complete! Yet, by midsummer, there was a new spirit in the man, marked by a confidence from which he never again retreated.

Of all the interpreters of Lincoln no one has expressed the change better than did the late Nathaniel W. Stephenson. "Out of this strange period of intolerable confusion," he wrote, "a gigantic figure had at last emerged. The outer and the inner Lincoln had fused. He was now a coherent personality, masterful in spite of his gentleness, with his own peculiar fashion of self-reliance, having a policy of his own devising, his colors nailed upon the masthead." We cannot, of course, know precisely what went on in Abraham Lincoln's soul in the dreadful winter of 1862, but we do know something of what emerged.

113

When President Lincoln was at the lowest point of his grief, in the late winter of 1862, one visitor to the White House made a lasting difference. This was Dr. Francis Vinton, rector of Trinity Church, New York. The insight that Dr. Smith had given the Lincolns in Springfield twelve years before was reaffirmed and made more intelligible by the spiritual help that Dr. Vinton offered the bereaved couple. His help came by the intellectual route, the only way in which it could come to Abraham Lincoln. The visitor showed that it is wholly rational for God to continue his interest in and concern for persons after the death of the body, just as before. Dr. Vinton called attention to Christ's own teaching on this point, especially as it is reported in Luke 20:38: "For he is not a God of the dead, but of the living: for all live unto him."

This approach seemed utterly fresh, as the rector of Trinity expounded it. Lincoln was struck especially by the visitor's confident words, "Your son is *alive*." As the president pondered, his entire outlook began to change for he realized that God cannot be defeated. If God cannot be defeated by the death of a little boy, it is also true that he cannot be defeated by a civil war. Ida Tarbell's insight at this point is as follows: "It was the first experience of his life, so far as we know, which drove him to look outside of his own mind and heart for help to endure a personal grief. It was the first time in his life when he had not been sufficient for his own experience." If there had not been the darkness of the late winter of 1862, it is not likely that there would have been the amazing burst of light at the end of the year. As he had done before, Lincoln matured best in sorrow. The profound paradox is that the great man became more confident in his approach to other men, including the men of his own cabinet, when he recognized that his major confidence was not in himself but in another.

That the new and stronger mood was the result of a fundamentally mystical experience is the conviction of one of the most thorough of Lincoln scholars, the late Nathaniel Stephenson. "Lincoln's final emergence," he says, "was a deeper thing than merely the consolidation of a character, the transformation of a dreamer into a man of action. The fusion of the outer and the inner person was the result of a profound interior change. Those elements of mysticism which were in him from the first, which had gleamed daily through such deep overshadowing, were at last established in their permanent form."

An Instrument of God's Will

Central to the new spiritual development was an enlargement of the idea of vocation. Less and less did the president think that he was acting merely in his own will or depending upon his own meager resources. "Hate, fear, jealousy," as Sandburg put it, "were rampant" in the summer, but that was not by any means the total story, for Lincoln grew immeasurably as he came to think of himself as an "instrument" of God's will. He needed an idea of this magnitude to keep him going in the face of unjust criticism as well as of military defeat. The sense that there really is a Guiding Hand, which makes possible a genuine calling for both individuals and nations, gave a tremendous new sense of moral strength. It was not enough to watch events and to muddle along day by day. What was much more important, Lincoln came to believe, was the effort to discern a pattern beneath the seeming irrationality of events. He had come really to believe that God molds history and that he employs erring mortals to effect his purpose.

The final position of political mysticism that Lincoln reached as a solution of his intellectual problem was equally removed from two extreme positions. On the one hand, it was far removed from the arrogant nationalism that assumes that God is on our side. Lincoln's concern, he said, was whether he was on God's side. He did not identify the will of his own fallible administration with the will of almighty God, because he saw everything, including his own presidency, proceeding under judgment. On the other hand, Lincoln did not admire those who think it is a mark of sophistication to sneer at patriotism. He believed that God has a will for a country and that an honest man should rejoice in the effort to try to remake his country after the divine pattern, insofar as this pattern is revealed to him. He loved his country devoutly; he believed it had been brought into existence for a purpose; he believed that this purpose had something to do with the ultimate welfare of mankind.

The Importance of the American Experiment

Before entering the White House, Lincoln had understood the evil character of human slavery, but in the agonizing months that followed his inauguration he came to see a still bigger issue, of which the slavery issue was only one part. This was the issue of the perpetuation of the ideal of democracy. As 1862 wore on, the sharpening of the intellectual position became more evident until it reached a climax in the message to Congress on December 1. What Lincoln was producing, in the months when some thought that he was doing very little, was an intellectual and spiritual clarification of the importance, for the whole world, of the American experiment in government.

On July 1 the president made a call for three hundred thousand three-year men, convinced by this time that the struggle would be long and that capitulation was out of the question. Already, on June 28, in a letter sent through Secretary William Seward to the Union governors meeting in New York, Lincoln indicated the firmness of his own resolve. "I expect," he said, "to maintain this contest until successful or until I die, or am conquered, or my term expires, or Congress or the country forsakes me."

116

On Sunday, July 13, riding in a carriage on the way to a funeral in the country near Washington, Lincoln confided to Secretary Welles and Secretary Seward his decision to issue a proclamation. Up to that time he had hesitated, in spite of much pressure, because of his great respect for the Constitution. He could not see how the Constitution could permit interference with practices that were legal in particular states. Now he had come to the momentous conclusion that emancipation could be declared on the ground of military necessity since, as commander in chief, the Constitution laid upon him the protection of the integrity of the country. An amendment to the Constitution could come later, but military necessity could be appealed to prior to the enactment of such an amendment. This is why the Emancipation Proclamation, when issued, freed slaves only in those areas engaged in open rebellion. To go further and to emancipate slaves in the border states would have been unconstitutional, since such action would not have been covered by the war powers of the president.

The famous proclamation, which the president had for so long contemplated in solitude, was read in its preliminary form to the cabinet on July 22, 1862. Except for Secretaries Welles and Seward, this came to the cabinet as a surprise. The president's style, they found, had radically altered. He did not ask for advice, the decision having been made.

The Influence of a Quaker Widow

In a year filled with important decisions and encounters, one event that contributed greatly to the final outcome occurred on Sunday morning, October 26. At that time Lincoln was visited by Eliza Gurney and a few others who sought to share with the president in the bearing of his burdens. What was originally understood by Lincoln as an ordinary interview turned out to be a genuine time of

117

worship. Even though the publication of the Emancipation Proclamation had already occurred, October was a very dark time. Oliver P. Morton, the wartime Governor of Indiana wrote to the president, "Another three months like the last six and we are lost—lost."

Eliza Gurney (1801–1881) was the widow of the famous English banker and Quaker minister, Joseph John Gurney. Although she was an American by birth, President Lincoln at first took her to be English. She had lived in England, at Earlham Hall, Norwich, until her husband's death, after which she returned to her native land. Like any sensitive person, Mrs. Gurney was deeply wounded by the sorrows of the Civil War and felt especial sympathy for President Lincoln in his position of awesome responsibility. Accordingly, she was led, in October 1862, to try to pay what she called a "religious visit" to the president, being accompanied on this visit by three other Friends, John M. Whitall, Hannah B. Mott, and James Carey. Not one of these sought anything for himself or herself, and none came either to criticize or to offer unasked advice. Because they came only to give spiritual support to one who sorely needed it, the president responded with unusual warmth. Consequently, he encouraged his visitors to stay much longer than the fifteen minutes originally intended, sharing with them in both silence and prayer.

"It was on the morning of the first day of the week, in a beating rain, that the little party repaired to the White House, where they were at once introduced into the private apartment of President Lincoln. . . . Deep thoughtfulness and intense anxiety marked his countenance, and created involuntary sympathy for him in this great national crisis." The participants left a careful account of what occurred. They spoke of "the almost awful silence," which moved the president deeply. He was accustomed to hearing words, many of them boring, but he was not accustomed to group silence. "The tears," we are told, "ran down his cheeks," and when vocal prayer was offered, "he reverently bowed his head."

After a time of silence Mrs. Gurney gave what was, in essence, a short sermon, which is reproduced in the Lincoln Papers. At the close of her sermon she knelt "and uttered a short but most beautiful, eloquent and comprehensive prayer that light and wisdom might be shed down from on high, to guide our President." After some further silence Lincoln himself spoke, uttering one of the most revealing messages of his entire career. While he obviously had no notes, and could not have had any advance intimation of what his visitors would say or do, the message turned out to be a remarkably finished one. This was possible because what he said was really a summary of what had been developing in his thought during more than a year of intellectual and spiritual struggle. The "instrument" theme here receives its finest expression.

> We are indeed going through a great trial—a fiery trial. In the very responsible position in which I happen to be placed, being a humble instrument in the hands of our Heavenly Father, as I am, and as we all are, to work out his great purposes, I have desired that all my works and acts may be according to his will, and that it might be so, I have sought his aid—but if after endeavoring to do my best in the light which he affords me, I find my efforts fail, I must believe that for some purpose unknown to me, He wills it otherwise. If I had had my way, this war would never have been commenced; if I had been allowed my way this war would have been ended before this, but we find it still continues; and we must believe that He permits it for some wise purpose of His own, mysterious and unknown to us; and though with our limited understandings we may not be able to comprehend it, yet we cannot but believe, that He who made the world still governs it.

119

The influence of Eliza Gurney on Lincoln's spiritual development is much more profound than has usually been recognized by Lincoln interpreters. Some biographers do not even mention her! Of especial interest is the fact that President Lincoln asked Mrs. Gurney to write to him, the request being transmitted through Isaac Newton, United States Commissioner of Agriculture. The president did this because he felt the need of spiritual support and had found a person who, without a trace of self-seeking, was able to give it. Accordingly, Mrs. Gurney wrote on August 18, 1863, from her new home in Atlantic City. The president's letter of September 4, 1864, was his response. In this it is important to remember he referred gratefully to the shared worship in the White House. "I have not forgotten—probably never shall forget—" he wrote, "the very impressive occasion when yourself and friends visited me on a Sabbath forenoon two years ago."

The Lincoln-Gurney letters, taken along with the "Meditation on the Divine Will," provide a genuine introduction to the theme completed in the Second Inaugural. The organ tones of that utterance are already suggested in Lincoln's letter to Mrs. Gurney, especially in the sentence, "The purposes of the Almighty are perfect, and must prevail, though we erring mortals may fail to accurately perceive them in advance." The expressions of the Second Inaugural would not have seemed novel to hearers if they had been able to read in advance the letters that passed between the struggling president and the widow of Joseph John Gurney. Most notable of all in Lincoln's letter is the near-perfect style of the sentence, "Surely He intends some great good to follow this mighty convulsion which no mortal could make, and no mortal could stay."

Calm in the Midst of the Storm

However long we face it, the miracle of Lincoln never ceases to astound us. How can it be that a person devoid of the advantages of a formal education should achieve such perfection of written and spoken style? As was true at Gettysburg, however memorable the deeds may have been, the words were more memorable still. When Lincoln said "The world will little note, nor long remember, what we say here, but it can never forget what they did here," he was being gloriously inaccurate.

It is fortunate that the leader of the nation in its time of greatest internal division was a thinker as well as a politician. As the agonizing months wore on, he saw, increasingly, that there could not be a merely military solution of the conflict. Union was one idea and emancipation was another, but he came to see the intricacy with which these two conceptions were intertwined. The way in which the Emancipation Proclamation was originated, developed, and superbly timed, far from being accidental, was the product of reasoning concerning both order and justice.

The real climax of the year of decision came one month before 1862 was ended, in Lincoln's message to Congress. In this utterance there appears the true character of the final plateau. "And while," Lincoln began, "it has not pleased the Almighty to bless us with a return of peace, we can but press on guided by the best light He gives us." This was not calm after the storm; it was calm in the midst of storm.

The Moral Pattern of History

John Bright is remembered for his influence upon American history, both in the way he helped to avoid armed conflict between Britain and America, and also in the way he prevented the recognition of the Confederacy by Great Britain and France. But many who are familiar with the work of Bright as a statesman are not equally familiar with the work of Bright as a thinker who influenced the mind of Abraham Lincoln. The fact that most of the connection

121

was through Charles Sumner, as an intermediary, does not lessen the importance of the impact. In Bright Lincoln found a true model, an astute statesman, who, like himself, had a pervading sense of the sovereignty of God. Bright's clearest statement of this position was made at Birmingham, on December 18, 1862, at the end of Lincoln's most agonizing year. "I believe," he said,

> the question is in the hand, not of my hon. Friend, nor in that of Lord Palmerston, nor in that even of President Lincoln, but it is in the hand of the Supreme Ruler, who is bringing about one of those great transactions in history which men often will not regard when they are passing before them, but which they look back upon with awe and astonishment some years after they are past.

As Bright indicated, and as Lincoln knew very well, it is difficult to look forward and see where the Guiding Hand is leading. But, seen in later perspective, the working out of a plan is sometimes obvious. Now enough years have elapsed for us, who belong to another generation, to see something of the pattern that was developing, in spite of the inadequacy of the human instruments when these responsible men lived and made decisions that affected the destinies of millions of people then unborn. What is truly remarkable is the way in which John Bright and Abraham Lincoln could see with so much perspective even while the events were transpiring. In the midst of history they partly discerned the meaning of that history.

To question, as some have done, whether Lincoln believed in God is a clear waste of time and effort. The answer is obvious. The only valuable inquiry is that of *how* he believed. In this regard the president grew prodigiously, and in this growth John Bright was one of his many teachers. Among other things, Bright helped by his emphasis upon moral consequences. As Bright looked at history he was convinced, as had been the major prophets of Israel, that God's hand in the course of events is seen in the working out of an objective moral law. A sin as great as the sin of enslaving other people was bound, thought Bright, to have agonizing consequences for a very long time. "Is not this war," he asked, "the penalty which inexorable justice exacts from America, North and South, for the enormous guilt of cherishing that frightful iniquity of slavery, for the last eighty years?"

When we consider Bright's question carefully, we are prepared to understand why Lincoln may be truly called the theologian of American anguish. The prairie lawyer answered Bright's question in the affirmative, haltingly at first, but finally with amazing firmness. He grew convinced that our universe, far from demonstrating a merely mechanical order, is a theater for the working out of the moral law. If he were alive today he would not be surprised at the continued agony that marks the relationships of black people and white people, not only in America, but also in many other parts of the world. The mills of the moral order, he thought, grind slowly, but they grind relentlessly. Slavery was a sin so terrible that men and women may still be paying for it a hundred years from now.

Lincoln was not, of course, alone in his understanding of the moral pattern of history with its consequent sorrow. Few who have understood the idea of providence have spoken primarily of comfort. Lincoln's correspondent, Eliza Gurney, spoke to him not only of the ecstasy, but also of the agony. "By terrible things in righteousness," she wrote, "the Lord seems indeed to have been answering our prayers that He would make us wholly His own."

More than a hundred years earlier, John Woolman, in the midst of his 1746 visit to colonies where the slave trade was common, wrote in his journal, "I Saw in these Southern Provinces, so many Vices and Corruptions increased by this trade and this way of life, that it appeared to me as a dark gloominess hanging over the Land, and though now many willingly run into it, yet in future the Consequence will be grievous to posterity." And then, to make sure that the reader would not suppose that the journalist was expressing a temporary emotion, Woolman added, "I express it as it hath appeared to me, not at once, nor twice, but as a matter fixed on my mind." Indeed, Woolman believed that the high cost of slavery, not only for the slaves, but also for owners and for the entire nation, would with the ensuing years grow greater rather than less. In 1757 he said, "I believe that burthen will grow heavier and heavier, till times change in a way disagreeable to us."

The events of Lincoln's administration were verifications of the truth of Woolman's remarkable prediction more than a century earlier. With Woolman and with Mrs. Gurney, Abraham Lincoln understood the concept of "terrible things in righteousness," because, like them, he knew Psalm 65:5.

A Rare Combination

One significant aspect of Lincoln's emphasis upon God's will was his complete lack of self-righteousness. In this he was remarkably different from many of his contemporaries, especially the extreme idealists who seemed to suppose that instant Utopia was possible. He differed from the fanatical moralists primarily in that he was always perplexed. No sooner did he believe that he was doing God's will than he began to admit that God's purpose might be different from his own. In short, he never forgot the immense contrast between the absolute goodness of God and the faltering goodness of all who are in the finite predicament. It was his recognition of the universality of human fallibility that made him conscious of the dangers involved in any governmental process, including the most democratic one. There is, he saw, no possible insurance against human error. His skepticism referred even to the judicial system, which is evident from his consideration of the Dred Scott decision. Indeed, as early as July 17, 1858, he quoted Thomas Jefferson with approbation on this very point. Jefferson's words, as Lincoln quoted them, were: "Our judges are as honest as other men, and not more so. They have, with others, the same passions for party, for power, and the privilege of their corps."

Always, in Lincoln's matured theology, there is paradox. There is sternness, yet there is also tenderness; there is melancholy, yet there is also humor; there is moral law, yet there is also compassion. History is the scene of the working out of God's justice, which we can never escape, but it is also the scene of the revelation of the everlasting mercy. Lincoln knew that if we stress only the mercy, we become sentimentalists, while, if we stress only the justice, we are driven to despair. The secret of rationality is the maintenance of the tension. The greatest possible mistake is the fatuous supposition that we have resolved it.

Scholars have noted in the passage from the Second Inaugural quoted above that the words succeed in expressing both the pious and the skeptical notes in Lincoln's matured faith. Reinhold Niebuhr drew attention to the reason why both notes were required, if the truth was to be told. Both are needed, he explained, because "the drama of history is shot through with moral meaning; but the meaning is never exact. Sin and punishment, virtue and reward are never precisely proportioned." Lincoln believed in providence, but, in Niebuhr's terms, he understood "the error of identifying providence with the cause to which the agent is committed."

When dedicated people forget the ubiquity of this danger, they are almost sure to become self-righteous. Only the person who recognizes that he is personally involved in the evils that he seeks to eliminate has any chance of avoiding this primary moral mistake. Lincoln, conscious as he was of the radical difference between the divine will and the human will, understood that ambiguities appear in the moral stance of even the most dedicated crusaders.

The character of Lincoln's intellectual achievement is better appreciated when we recognize that the combination that he demonstrated is exceedingly rare. There are many instances in history of people who allow their skepticism to cut the nerve of moral effort, and there are numerous people, on the other hand, who are fierce crusaders at the price of fanaticism. In his political commitments the fanatic makes claims for his particular cause that cannot be validated by either a transcendent providence or a neutral posterity.

Lincoln's achievement looms the greater in our own years, since they are marked almost as much by anguish as were his own. The more we observe the failure of the obvious alternatives, i.e., spirituality without passion, and passion without perspective, the more we realize the real brilliance of Lincoln's mature solution of the problem. "It was," said Niebuhr, "Lincoln's achievement to embrace a paradox which lies at the center of the spirituality of all western culture; namely, the affirmation of a meaningful history and the religious reservation about the partiality and bias which the human actors and agents betray in the definition of meaning." Both Abraham Lincoln and Jefferson Davis were patriotic and also reverent men, but there was a crucial difference between them, because Lincoln appreciated paradox as Jefferson Davis did not.

An American Vision

Abraham Lincoln was a patriot who was devoted to something far more profound than what is ordinarily understood as nationalism. America was important in his eyes because God, he believed, had a magnificent work for America to perform, a work significant for the whole world. This, as he said at Trenton before his first inauguration, was "something that held out a great promise to all the people of the world to all time to come." In calling Americans to this vision of greatness God might even go so far, he thought, as to *compel* obedience. In this conviction Lincoln's mood was similar to that of some of the Old Testament prophets. In June 1862, the crucial month for making up his mind whether to issue the Emancipation Proclamation, he had an important confrontation with a group brought to him by James F. Wilson, Iowa congressman and chairman of the House Judiciary Committee.

One member of Wilson's delegation, a strong antislavery man, said to the president, "Slavery must be stricken down wherever it exists. If we do not do right I believe God will let us go our own way to our ruin. But if we do right I believe he will lead us safely out of this wilderness, crown our arms with victory, and restore our now disseevered Union."

The significance of Lincoln's response lies in the way in which he picked up the man's idea of divine guidance and went beyond it. He rose slowly to his full height, "his right arm outstretched toward the gentleman who had just ceased speaking, his face aglow like the face of a prophet," reported the congressman. To the surprise of his admonisher the president said, "My faith is greater than yours." In common with his visitor, he, too, believed in the role of God in history, but he went on to declare a new thing, to the effect that God will not abandon us to the foolishness of our own devices. "I also believe," he continued, "that He will compel us to do right in order that He may do these things, not so much because we desire them as that they accord with His plan of dealing with this nation, in the midst of which He means to establish justice. I think He means that we shall do more than we have yet done in furtherance of His plans, and He will open the way for our doing it. I have felt His hand upon me in great trials and

127

submitted to His guidance, and I trust that as He shall further open the way, I will be ready to walk therein, relying on His help and trusting in His goodness and wisdom."

One of the most revealing features of Lincoln's Second Inaugural is its intimation of what his policy would have been after the war, if he had survived. He would have treated Southerners as though they had never left the Union. One who saw this clearly was Sir Winston Churchill, who pointed out that "the death of Lincoln deprived the Union of the guiding hand which alone could have solved the problems of reconstruction and added to the triumph of armies those lasting victories which are gained over the hearts of men." At the cabinet meeting on April 14, 1865, the very day on which he was shot, the president spoke of Robert E. Lee and other Confederate leaders with kindness. The assassin's bullet hurt the entire nation, but it hurt the southern part of the nation most of all. In Lincoln's last public address, given on April 11, 1865, three days before the assassination, he spoke directly of reconstruction after the war, saying that the problems it presented had pressed closely upon his attention. Then, in one of his laconic sentences, he added, "It is fraught with great difficulty."

Nothing in Lincoln's theology made him expect Utopia. He did not claim that the victory of the Union forces would necessarily produce the full liberation of people, black and white. All that he claimed was that such a victory would provide *opportunity*, while defeat would entail unmitigated disaster. He accepted the basic philosophy of the founding fathers, including the idea of a special destiny for America, but he was sufficiently acquainted with human failure to know that progress is never certain, as it is never easy. His only certainty lay in the conviction that God will never cease to call America to her true service, not only for her own sake but for the sake of the world. He desired unity and he knew that vision is the secret of unity. Consequently, his final appeal was for the completion of what he interpreted as a holy calling. This is the significance of the admonition, "Let us strive on to finish the work we are in." Knowing that the American experiment was incomplete, he was keenly aware of the appeal produced by any structure that is only partly finished and that, accordingly, cries out for completion. He did not predict an end to American anguish, but he did see the possibility of a determination "to do all which may achieve and cherish a just, and a lasting peace, among ourselves, and with all nations."

The Gettysburg Address

November 19, 1863

Fourscore and seven years ago our fathers brought forth on this continent a new nation, conceived in liberty and dedicated to the proposition that all men are created equal. Now we are engaged in a great civil war, testing whether that nation or any nation so conceived and so dedicated can long endure. We are met on a great battlefield of that war. We have come to dedicate a portion of that field as a final resting-place for those who here gave their lives that that nation might live. It is altogether fitting and proper that we should do this. But in a larger sense, we cannot dedicate, we cannot consecrate, we cannot hallow this ground. The brave men, living and dead who struggled here have consecrated it far above our poor power to add or detract. The world will little note nor long remember what we say here, but it can never forget what they did here. It is for us the living rather to be dedicated here to the unfinished work which they who fought here have thus far so nobly advanced. It is rather for us to be here dedicated to the great task remaining before us—that from these honored dead we take increased devotion to that cause for which they gave the last full measure of devotion—that we here highly resolve that these dead shall not have died in vain, that this nation under God shall have a new birth of freedom, and that government of the people, by the people, for the people shall not perish from the earth.

Second Inaugural Address

March 4, 1865

At this second appearing to take the oath of the Presidential office there is less occasion for an extended address than there was at the first. Then, a statement somewhat in detail of a course to be pursued seemed fitting and proper. Now, at the expiration of four years, during which public declarations have been constantly called forth on every point and phase of the great contest which still absorbs the attention and engrosses the energies of the nation, little that is new would be presented. The progress of our arms, upon which all else chiefly depends, is as well known to the public as to myself, and it is, I trust, reasonably satisfactory and encouraging to all. With high hope for the future, no prediction in regard to it is ventured.

On the occasion corresponding to this, four years ago all thoughts were anxiously directed to an impending civil war. All dreaded it, all sought to avert it. While the inaugural address was being delivered from this place, devoted altogether to saving the Union without war, insurgent agents were in the city seeking to destroy it without war, seeking to dissolve the Union and divide effects by negotiation. Both parties deprecated war, but one of them would make war rather than let the nation survive, and the other would accept war rather than let it perish, and the war came.

One-eighth of the whole population were colored slaves, not distributed generally over the Union, but localized in the southern part of it. These slaves constituted a peculiar and powerful interest. All knew that this interest was somehow the cause of the war. To strengthen, perpetuate, and extend this interest was the object for which the insurgents would rend the Union, even by war; while the Government claimed no right to do more than to restrict the territorial enlargement of it. Neither party expected for the war the magnitude or the duration which it has already attained. Neither anticipated that the cause of the conflict might cease with, or even before, the conflict itself should cease. Each looked for an easier triumph, and a result less fundamental and astounding. Both read the same Bible and pray to the same God, and each invoked His aid against the other. It may seem strange that any men should dare to ask a just God's assistance in wringing their bread from the sweat of other men's faces, but let us judge not, that we be not judged. The prayers of both could not be answered. That of neither has been answered fully. The Almighty has His own purposes. "Woe unto the world because of offenses; for it must needs be that offenses come, but woe to that man by whom the offense cometh." If we shall suppose that American slavery is one of those offenses which, in the providence of God, must needs come, but which, having continued through His appointed time, He now wills to remove, and that He gives to both North and South this terrible war as the woe due to those by whom the offense came, shall we discern therein any departure from those divine attributes which the believers in a living God always ascribe to Him? Fondly do we hope, fervently do we pray, that this mighty scourge of war may speedily pass away. Yet, if God wills that it continue until all the wealth piled by the bondsman's two hundred and fifty years of unrequited toil shall be sunk, and until every drop of blood drawn with the lash shall be paid by another drawn with the sword, as was said three thousand years ago, so still it must be said "the judgments of the Lord are true and righteous altogether."

With malice toward none, with charity for all, with firmness in the right as God gives us to see the right, let us strive on to finish the work we are in, to bind up the nation's wounds, to care for him who shall have borne the battle and for his widow and his orphan, to do all which may achieve and cherish a just and lasting peace among ourselves and with all nations.

Aleksandr I. Solzhenitsyn

The Writer Underground

Alonzo L. McDonald

The Soviet Union is no more. It has splintered into more than a dozen divisive entities. The reign of absolute authoritarianism in government, brutal and vicious disregard and degradation of human beings in everyday life, and atheism in spirit has collapsed of internal rot. The centralized administration of minimum material equality in lieu of individual choice and initiative has dissipated the vast wealth of an enormous and powerful empire populated by a noble, proud, and potentially productive people.

It is tempting now to forget the massive horrors and endless acts of inhumanity perpetrated by one of history's most vicious totalitarian regimes. Our normal Western tendency is to overlook even the present, filling our thoughts with the future. But in this instance, the lessons of the past should not be readily forgotten. In the short space of the twentieth century, after the world's full realization of the shocking impact of the Nazi Holocaust, we see on an even more massive scale the capacity of human beings to denigrate the value and meaning of life and to put to death three score and ten million human beings.

The following excerpts from Solzhenitsyn's *The Oak and the Calf* can only serve as brief reminders of this tragedy of oppression. Yet, directly or between the lines, his thoughts also encompass a spectrum of other lessons that we who strive to live rich and full lives should repeatedly ponder. These lessons relate to the human spirit, matters of the soul, and the dimensions of a personal relationship with one's Creator that enabled a single individual—an imprisoned and exiled unknown writer often without even pen or paper—to wreak havoc on an all-powerful earthly system based on massive material supremacy and an awesome array of brute military and police force.

It is well worth our time to reflect on our own individual lives, our unique missions in this world, our personal spiritual balance, and our everyday moral values. Even from the depths of the human condition, as Solzhenitsyn has witnessed, each of us has the choice also to turn our gaze upward.

The Man

The life of Aleksandr Isayevich Solzhenitsyn is as complex, mysterious, eventful, and challenging to understand as his major writings. To encapsulate his life is by definition to do it injustice. Yet even a glimpse can serve as an inspiration for those of us who struggle through the tedium of living in a relatively free society, searching out and choosing meanings for our lives. As in the case of other great individuals with a strong, spiritual commitment, we can only take encouragement from those who have met the test and by most standards excelled.

Solzhenitsyn has been both praised and virulently criticized in the East and the West. Even while documenting the atrocities of the Soviet Union in massive detail, he refused to become a political pawn. Instead he looked beyond the superpowers' struggle to express historical perspectives on the grander human spirit and its resilience.

In his famous Harvard commencement address of 1978, Solzhenitsyn criticized vehemently the materialism, greed, and declining courage and moral values of the West. He observed that the Western democracies were concerned more with the letter of the law—to be historically significant mainly as a juridical society—rather than with justice, truth, or the realization of human potential under God. He was particularly critical of the media, charging it with inaccuracy, guesswork, superficiality, sensationalism, and misleading judgments—all without accountability or rectification.

"After the suffering of decades of violence and oppression, the human soul longs for things higher, warmer, and purer than those offered by today's mass living habits, introduced by the revolting invasion of publicity, by TV stupor, and by intolerable music," he lamented. He concluded that spiritual life was destroyed in the East by the ruling party and in the West by commercial interests. Thus, although socialism was despicable, he could not recommend the system of the West to his fellow Russians either.

Naturally, his critics multiplied as his writings threatened almost all special and powerful interests—including church leaders and pacifists in the West—whom he accused of knowing of nothing in life worth dying for. If his critics registered at all with Solzhenitsyn, they deterred him in no way from pursuing his mission of chronicling the miseries, sacrifices, and spiritual challenges of his brothers and sisters in bondage.

Although Solzhenitsyn decries most biographical efforts as a waste of his time, we know much about him and his life. He was born in December of 1918 in a small health resort in the northern Caucasus. His birth came six months after his father's accidental death in a hunting accident, incurred while recuperating from wounds received as a thrice-decorated Russian artilleryman on the German front in World War I.

137

Solzhenitsyn's mother and father were married at the front in 1917 and had lived together less than a year, struggling as a young couple to recover his father's health and to find a viable place in the extreme disorder following the Russian Revolution.

The widow and her small son moved to Rostov-on-Don when he was six, where she struggled to find periodic work as a typist and stenographer to support them. She never remarried but lived a hard, devoted life until her death from tuberculosis in 1944. Solzhenitsyn was serving on the Western front in the Russian army at this time.

Solzhenitsyn wanted to write from about the age of nine but lamented that he could not find things to write about. Even so, he scribbled out items that he later described as "only rubbish." Yet, even in his early years he developed a disciplined approach to writing that called him to work incessantly at putting down his thoughts and ideas in various forms, from poetry to prose.

Finishing his secondary education in 1936, Solzhenitsyn dreamed of higher education in literature but found the faculty at Rostov University below his standards. He therefore entered its department of physics and mathematics, graduating in 1941 after having earned one of the early Stalin scholarships, which carried a hefty stipend that helped enormously to support both him and his mother.

His mastery of mathematics came frequently to his aid in later life—in the structure and architecture of his writings, in the systematic handling of his personal affairs, in his rise to become an artillery officer, in obtaining a special assignment during half of his prison term as a mathematician in a security police research center, and in exile by finding employment as a mathematics teacher in the isolated town of Berlik much nearer the Chinese border than to Moscow. He did take several literary courses by correspondence from the noted Moscow Institute of Philosophy, Literature, and History, but after his first three semesters the Institute was closed because of its freethinking inclinations, thus ending his literary studies.

Solzhenitsyn married in 1940 but left shortly afterward as a private in the army. Here his mathematical training helped him to complete a crash course at artillery school and become an officer. He rose to become the commander of a reconnaissance battery, was twice decorated, and remained continuously at the front throughout 1943 and 1944 until he was arrested in February of 1945 while advancing with his troops into Germany. Because he had criticized Stalin in correspondence with an old friend, he was tried and sentenced to eight years in a labor camp in the Arctic islands. He ultimately served his full term, about half as a laborer, bricklayer, and a foundry worker before he was assigned as a mathematician. This move certainly helped him survive that depraved experience.

After completing his sentence in 1953, Solzhenitsyn was sent "permanently into exile," far from Russia to the desert steppes of Kazakhstan. In a stroke of good fortune he obtained employment as a secondary schoolteacher at great risk to the local official who hired him.

During his imprisonment Solzhenitsyn had come down with intestinal cancer and was subjected to a crude operation. Shortly after arriving in exile his condition worsened, and he almost died before finding medical help. He made contact with a naturalist working with herbs about a hundred miles away, a dangerous unauthorized journey away from his exile post. This mountain man gave him small doses of poisonous herbs that sufficiently arrested the cancer's progress until he could get clearance to go to a hospital in Tashkent. The agony of waiting through all these experiences and administrative delays was enough to test the will to live of any human being, much less one's dedication to a personal mission.

At the Tashkent hospital, which became the scene of his novel *Cancer Ward*, he was subjected to X-ray treatments and began to improve. He later attributed his recuperation to "a divine miracle." This reinforced his faith, which had become a dominant part of his life in prison as he gradually converted his commitment from Marxism to Christianity.

After the initial publication of *One Day in the Life of Ivan Denisovich*, published only under the direct instructions of Nikita Khrushchev, his later writings were largely refused publication as the hardliners regained control. In the meantime he had become famous overnight for that one story and was continually badgered by the KGB and fellow writers, finally being ousted from the Soviet Writers' Union and essentially banned from any further publication in his homeland.

Following some political easing in 1956 he was finally released from exile. His record still made him a "counter revolutionary," leaving him essentially an untouchable within Soviet society. For another nine months, during a short but fortunate window in one of the most liberal years in Soviet history during the anti-Stalin crusade, he worked his way through the bureaucratic snares encompassing his prison sentence to win a ruling on February 6, 1957, from the Supreme Court of the USSR exonerating him and dismissing his case. Afterward, from a legal perspective, his résumé seemed highly attractive as a student, frontline officer, and teacher. He could skip any further references to his arrest, his prison service, or his time of exile.

In 1973 he wrote a scathing letter to the Soviet leadership that the state simply could not ignore. The KGB increased its pressure, arresting a typist who had been entrusted with one copy of *The Gulag Archipelago*. After some five days of questioning day and night, she confessed its location from which the authorities retrieved it. Upon being released she went home and committed suicide.

Solzhenitsyn immediately authorized publication of *Gulag* outside of Russia. This book is a massive indictment of all Russians, holding them accountable for the accumulated crimes of the state.

The government could no longer tolerate his challenges. In February he was twice ordered to appear before state prosecutors. In those instances he ignored the court orders because "of the complete and general illegality ruling in our country for many years." On February 13, 1974, he was arrested by the KGB and held for some twenty-four hours before being deprived of citizenship and flown against his will to Frankfurt.

Solzhenitsyn's deportation became a major international news story. He was deluged by the media, which he soon detested, claiming that an intrusive mob of photographers "were even worse than the KGB." He initially settled in Zürich but later moved on to Vermont. He has spent much of his time since that era writing on later stages of his master work, *The Red Wheel*, which he has indicated will take approximately twenty years to complete.

His Writings

Solzhenitsyn's writings were not intended as political commentary but rather as expressions of universal moral values. To the dismay of Western writers and critics he refused to be used as an anti-Soviet propagandist, persistently striving to document thoroughly an ignoble period in Russian history.

Although his major writings were refused publication in the USSR following *Ivan Denisovich*, Solzhenitsyn allowed publication of *Cancer Ward* in the West in 1968. He was then awarded the Nobel Prize for literature for "the ethical force with which he has pursued the indispensable tradition of Russian literature." Fearing deportation, he would

141

not leave his country to accept the award at the time, but did so later after his forced flight to the West. In 1971 he allowed publication of *August 1914*, a massive work that reportedly took some twenty years to complete. It centered around Tannenburg, where his father had fought in World War I, an area through which he had also marched as an officer in the Russian army in World War II.

The first two of seven parts to *The Gulag Archipelago* were published in December 1973 following increased pressures from the KGB and fears about manuscript seizures. After receiving death threats, he then went public with a press conference with Westerners in Moscow. This tended to protect him but also helped accelerate his government's deportation decision.

Solzhenitsyn continues writing to this day on a massive series of volumes. Although his two-thousand-page version of *The Gulag Archipelago* is overwhelming to most Westerners, critics have repeatedly pointed out that his writing is strictly for the Russian audience. It represents a historical documentation of an endless series of events rather than simply vivid novels for popular appeal. In *Gulag* he not only relied on his own experiences but incorporated materials he developed from long research and interviews with 227 other inmates. Their variety of horrors and experiences helped to complete the massive documentation of the sacrifices made by so many of his brother and sister "Zeks" in the infamous Arctic prison system.

His Calling

In the reading that follows, the continuing theme of a dedicated individual with truly a spiritual calling predominates his thoughts. They show the intensity with which he devoted himself to his work—even in prison, where the memorization of his work took one week of each month simply to repeat to himself the items previously composed.

Then, fighting all odds, he feared that all of this memory work would be lost with him through a cancerous death. To preserve what he could, he then scribbled his writings on tiny handwritten scrolls, inserted them in a champagne bottle, and buried it in the backyard of his residence in Berlik. He then left for Tashkent to enter the hospital where he expected to die.

For many, many years, Solzhenitsyn had no real hope that his work would be published, yet he persevered. Even when released from exile, there was a constant threat that the KGB would confiscate the pages of his compositions. Often there was only a single copy. Therefore secrecy and anonymity became major assets in pressing ahead with his work until the publication of *Ivan Denisovich* took him overnight from an unknown, secondary schoolteacher in the hinterlands to an instant celebrity, placing him also under constant KGB scrutiny.

Underlying all his work is the sense that he was called by God to record for history the terrible sacrifices of his fellow citizens. He let nothing stand in the way of this mission. As his life matured and his challenges became greater, he seemed to gain strength not only to pursue his writings but also to express openly his faith and his moral values.

Modern critics have difficulty dealing with this aspect of Solzhenitsyn's life and writings since it is no longer fashionable to talk about heroes or one's beliefs. In his own words, however, Solzhenitsyn speaks from the soul in a way that touches us all, forcing our personal reflections on the spiritual basis for our existence and the fundamental meaning of our own lives.

In 1972 Solzhenitsyn publicly declared his faith and released a poem written some ten years earlier in prison. It tells us much about this man who is surely a modern hero even in a hypercynical world.

> How easy it is to live with You, O Lord.
> How easy to believe in You.
> When my spirit is overwhelmed within me,
> When even the keenest see no further than the night,
> And know not what to do tomorrow,
> You bestow on me the certitude
> That You exist and are mindful of me,
> That all the paths of righteousness are not barred.
> As I ascend in to the hill of earthly glory,
> I turn back and gaze, astonished, on the road
> That led me here beyond despair,
> Where I too may reflect Your radiance upon mankind.
>
> All that I may reflect, You shall accord me,
> And appoint others where I shall fail.

Regardless of our individual beliefs, such devoted testimony and dedication behooves each of us to reflect again on our unique calling, our special mission on this earth.

The Oak and the Calf

Aleksandr I. Solzhenitsyn

The Writer Underground

Underground is where you expect to find revolutionaries. But not writers.

For the writer intent on truth, life never was, never is (and never will be!) easy: his like have suffered every imaginable harassment—defamation, duels, a shattered family life, financial ruin or lifelong unrelieved poverty, the madhouse, jail. . . .

I drifted into literature unthinkingly, without really knowing what I needed from it, or what I could do for it. I just felt depressed because it was so difficult, I thought, to find fresh subjects for stories. I hate to think what sort of writer I would have become (for I would have gone on writing) if I had not been *put inside*.

Once arrested, once I had spent two years in prisons and camps, depressed now by the mountainous overabundance of subjects, I accepted as effortlessly as the air I breathed, accepted with all the other unchallengeable realities before my eyes, the knowledge that not only would no one ever publish me, but a single line could cost me my life. Without hesitation, without inner debate, I entered into the inheritance of every modern Russian writer intent on the truth: I must write simply to ensure that it was not all forgotten, that posterity might someday come to know of it. Publication in my own lifetime I must shut out of my mind, out of my dreams.

I put away my idle dream. And in its place there was only the surety that my work would not be in vain, that it would someday smite the heads I had in my sights, and that those who received its invisible emanations would understand. I no more rebelled against lifelong silence than against the lifelong impossibility of freeing my feet from the pull of gravity. As I finished one piece after another, at first in camps, then in exile, then after rehabilitation, first verses, then plays, and later prose works too, I had only one desire: to keep all these things out of sight and myself with them.

In the camp this meant committing my verse—many thousands of lines—to memory. To help me with this I improvised decimal counting beads and, in transit prisons, broke up matchsticks and used the fragments as tallies. As I approached the end of my sentence I grew more confident of my powers of memory, and began writing down and memorizing prose—dialogue at first, but then, bit by bit, whole densely written passages. My memory found room for them! It worked. But more and more of my time—in the end as much as one week every month—went into the regular repetition of all I had memorized.

Life Given Back

Then came exile, and right at the beginning of my exile, cancer. In autumn 1953 it looked very much as though I had only a few months to live. In December the doctors—comrades in exile—confirmed that I had at most three weeks left.

All that I had memorized in the camps ran the risk of extinction together with the head that held it.

This was a dreadful moment in my life: to die on the threshold of freedom, to see all I had written, all that gave meaning to my life thus far, about to perish with me. The peculiarities of the Soviet postal censorship made it impossible for me to cry out for help: Come quickly, take what I have written, save it! You can't very well appeal to strangers anyway. My friends were all in camps themselves. My mother was dead. My wife had married again. All the same, I sent for her to say goodbye, thinking that she might take my manuscripts away with her, but she did not come. . . .

In those last few weeks that the doctors had promised me I could not escape from my work in school, but in the evening and at night, kept awake by pain, I hurriedly copied things out in tiny handwriting, rolled them, several pages at a time, into tight cylinders and squeezed these into a champagne bottle. I buried the bottle in my garden—and set off for Tashkent to meet the new year (1954) and to die.

I did not die, however. With a hopelessly neglected and acutely malignant tumor, this was a divine miracle; I could see no other explanation. Since then, all the life that has been given back to me has not been mine in the full sense: it is built around a purpose. . . .

The Book Is Mightier Than the Bullet

Later, by contrast, the pace slackened. Life dragged on like a lingering cold spring. History began to cast loop after nooselike loop of complications, hoping to lasso every one of us, and strangle as many as possible. Things moved so sluggishly (just as we should have expected) that we no longer had any choice: there was nothing for it but to hurl a few last stones, with our last remaining strength, at that impenetrable brow.

Yes, yes, of course—we all know that you cannot poke a stick through the walls of a concrete tower, but here's something to think about: what if those walls are only a painted backdrop?

Looking back, even a fool would be able to predict it today: the Soviet regime could certainly have been breached only by literature. The regime has been reinforced with concrete to such an extent that neither a military coup nor a political organization nor a picket line of strikers can knock it over or run it through. Only the solitary writer would be able to do this. And the Russian younger generation would move on into the breach.

Obvious? Yet no one foresaw it, either in the thirties or in the fifties. That's the trouble with the future: it slips away and eludes us. . . .

Shortly before his death Tolstoy wrote that it is always immoral for a writer to publish in his own lifetime. We should, he thinks, write only for the future, and let our works be published "posthumously." Tolstoy reached his pious conclusions on this as on all else only after making the full round of sins and passions, but in any case, what he says is untrue even for slower epochs, and still more so for our swift-moving times. He is right that the thirst for repeated successes with the public spoils a writer's work. But it is even more damaging to be denied readers for years on end—demanding readers, hostile readers, delighted readers—to be denied all opportunity to influence the world about you, to influence the rising generation, with your pen. Quiescence means purity—but also irresponsibility. Tolstoy's judgment is ill-considered. . . .

The Hidden Costs of Fame and Freedom

I started meeting people who had read my story. After the unbroken silence of my underground existence, two dozen such readers made me feel that the eyes of the crowd were on me, and my fame was growing dizzily.

I made hasty preparations for a new and dangerous stage in my life. It was one thing to hide manuscripts when I was one grain of sand among millions, quite another now that I had shown myself: the Lubyanka might be more persistently inquisitive than *Novy Mir* and send some of its hangers-on to make an unhurried search for anything else I might have written.

I began reviewing my hiding places, and they now seemed too obvious, too easily guessable by expert housebreakers. So I myself broke into some of them and destroyed their contents, eliminating every trace. I burned all superfluous drafts and rough copies. The rest I decided not to keep at home, and on the eve of 1962 my wife and I took all that I had spared of my archive to her friend Teush in Moscow. (It was this archive that the *oprichniki* would seize three and a half years later.)

I have a particularly vivid memory of this removal, by local train on New Year's Eve, because a drunken hooligan burst into the compartment and began abusing the passengers. It so happened that none of the men present tried to stop him: those who were not too old were too cautious. It would have been natural for me to jump up: I was sitting quite close, and I had the right sort of mug for the job. But the precious suitcase containing all my manuscripts stood at our feet, and I dared not move: if it came to a fight, I would inevitably have to tag along to the militia station, if only as a witness, either taking my suitcase with me or— just as bad—leaving it behind.

It would be a truly Russian happening if all my cunningly woven threads were snapped by this hooligan. So in order to fulfill my duty as a Russian, I had to exercise a quite un-Russian self-restraint. I sat there, feeling ashamed and cowardly, staring at the floor while the women scolded us for our unmanliness.

This was one of many times when my secret life as a writer robbed me—not always in such a humiliating way, but just as aggravatingly—of my freedom of action, my freedom to speak my mind, my freedom to stand up straight. We all had heavy loads on our backs, but I was also dragged down, and my spiritual energies diverted from literature, by unwieldy burdens hidden beneath the surface. My bones would ache with longing: Straighten up! Straighten up if you die for it!

"Don't Let Good Luck Fool You or Bad Luck Frighten You"

. . . I may say that my whole life has trained me to expect the worst much more often than not, and I am always readier, more willing to believe, the worst. In the camp I took to heart the Russian proverb: "Don't let good luck fool you or bad luck frighten you." I have learned to live by this rule, and I hope never to depart from it. . . .

If a deep-sea fish used to a constant pressure of many atmospheres rises to the surface, it perishes because it cannot adjust to excessively low pressures, and in much the same way I, who for fifteen years had lurked discreetly in the depths— the camps, exile, underground—never showing myself, never making a single noticeable mistake about a person or a situation, now that I had risen to the surface and to sudden fame, inordinately resounding fame (for in our country abuse and praise alike are always carried to extremes), began making blunder after blunder, completely failing to understand my new position and my new possibilities. . . .

"Why are you always in such a hurry?" I was in such a hurry because in my fifth decade I was bursting with all that remained to be written, and because falsehood stood only too firmly on its feet of clay—or rather its feet of reinforced concrete. . . .

In the autumn of 1963 I selected chapters from *The First Circle* and tried them on *Novy Mir*, calling them "a fragment."

Novy Mir rejected them. Because they were only a fragment? Not only that. This was "that prison theme again." (And the prison theme was exhausted, wasn't it? Already overdone?) This was just at the time when they had to print a summary of next year's publishing plans. I offered them my long tale *Cancer Ward,* which I was already writing. The title was quite unsuitable! To begin with, it smacked of allegory, and anyway, "It's too frightening in itself; it'll never get through."

Tvardovsky, who insisted on renaming everything submitted to *Novy Mir,* immediately decided on the new title: *"Patients and Doctors.* We'll put it in the prospectus."

Like a smear of porridge on a plate! *Patients and Doctors* . . . I wouldn't hear of it. If you have found the right title for a book, or even a short story, it isn't a mere label, it is part of the soul and essence of the thing, organically linked with it, and changing the title means mutilating the work itself.

Bolder by the Day

My plan was an immensely ambitious one; in another ten years time I should be ready to face the world with all that I had written, and I should not mind if I perished in the flames of that literary explosion—but now, just one slip of the foot, one careless move, and my whole plan, my whole life's work had come to grief. And it was not only my life's work but the dying wish of the millions whose last whisper, last moan, had been cut short on some hut floor in some prison camp. I had not carried out their behests, I had betrayed them, had shown myself unworthy of them. It had been given to me, almost alone, to crawl to safety; the hopes once held in all those skulls buried now in common graves in the camps had been set on me—and I collapsed, and their hopes had slipped from my hands. . . .

151

History moves in unexpected twists and turns. At one time we, the unlucky ones, were put inside for nothing, for half a word or a quarter of a seditious thought. Now the KGB had a whole bouquet of criminal charges to pin on me (according to their legal code, of course), yet this had only untied my hands, given me ideological extraterritoriality! Half a year after the event, it had become clear that the unhappy loss of my archives had brought me complete freedom of thought and of belief. I was free not merely to believe in God, although I was a member of the Marxist and atheist Writers' Union, but to profess any political view I chose. For nothing I might think now could be worse and harsher than the angry words in the play I had written in camp. If they weren't going to *put me inside* for that, they obviously wouldn't put me in for any of the beliefs I might come to hold. I could reply to my correspondents as frankly as I pleased, say whatever I liked in conversation, and none of it could be worse than my play! I could make whatever entries I pleased in my diaries: no more need to use code and subterfuge. I was approaching an invisible divide beyond which there was no more need for hypocrisy—about anything, or to anyone!

I concluded then, in spring 1966, that I had been given a lengthy reprieve, but I also realized the need for an *overt* and generally accessible work to proclaim in the meantime that I was alive and working, to occupy in the public mind the space that my confiscated works had not been able to invade.

Cancer Ward, which I had begun three years earlier, would be very suitable for this purpose. I set to work completing it.

The Cheka-KGB would not wait, it was not dozing, and haste was a tactical necessity. But how can you step up the pace of your writing? Then I had the idea of publishing Part One to start with, without waiting to finish Part Two. The tale itself did not call for this, but tactical necessity left me no room for maneuver.

Racing against Time

How I should have liked to work at my own speed! How I should have liked at least to take some time off from writing daily for unhurried and disinterested language exercises. How I longed to rewrite my text a dozen times, to put it aside and come back to it years later, and to examine rival candidates at length before inserting missing words. But my life always was, and still is, a race against time, my timetable impossibly tight; I am only too happy if I manage to sketch out the most urgent things! Sometimes I can't even do that. . . .

Many writers have had to write in a hurry—usually to fulfill their contracts, to meet deadlines. But you might think that I had no need to hurry, that I could polish and polish again. No. There were always powerful, compelling reasons—the need to hide, to disperse copies, to take advantage of someone's help, to set myself free for other tasks—so that I never released anything without undue haste, I never had time to look for the precise, the definitive words. . . .

The Curse of the KGB

This is a strange thing I seem to be producing. One not foreseen in my early plans and not essential to them. I can write it or leave it alone. For three years I have let it rest, well hidden. I didn't know whether I would ever care enough to come back to it. A few close friends read it and said there was life in it, that I should certainly go on. So, while I take a breather between the "Knots" [volumes] of my main book, I am immersing myself in this one again.

The first thing I see is that I ought not just to carry on where I left off, but to bring out more clearly, to explain more fully, this miracle: that I walk at my ease through marshes, stand firm upon the quaking bog, go dry-shod

153

over whirlpools, hover in midair without support. From outside it is not obvious how a man with the state's curse upon him and the KGB's hoops about him can fail to crack. How he can hold out single-handed, yes, and fork over mountains of work, find time now and then to root in archives and in libraries, to write around for information, to check quotations, to interview elderly people, to write, to type, to collate and bind copy after copy, as book after book goes into samizdat (and there is always another in reserve): Where do I get the strength? From what miraculous source?

To shirk the task of explaining is impossible, to find the right words still more so. Safer times will come, God grant, and then I shall fill the gaps. For the present I am afraid even to put the outline of an explanation on paper as an aid to memory, afraid that the scrap of paper may find its way to the Cheka-KGB.

But as I read over what I have written, I see that in the last few years I have grown stronger and braver, that I dare to put out my horns more and more often, that today I can bring myself to write things that three years ago seemed deadly dangerous. I see more and more clearly where my chosen trail is leading: to victory or destruction.

What makes this piece so strange is that for any other you draw up an architectural plan, you see the unwritten parts implicit in the whole, you try to make each part subserve the whole. But this book is an agglomeration of lean-tos and annexes, and there is no knowing how big the next addition will be, or where it will be put. At any point I can call the book finished or unfinished. I can abandon it or I can continue it as long as life goes on, or until the calf breaks its neck butting the oak, or until the oak cracks and comes crashing down.

An unlikely happening, but one in which I am very ready to believe. . . .

Waiting for the Great Outcry

From dawn to dusk the correction and copying of *Gulag* went forward; I could scarcely keep the pages moving fast enough. Then the typewriter started breaking down every day, and I had either to solder it myself or take it to be repaired. This was the most frightening moment of all: we had the only original manuscript and all the typed copies of *Gulag* there with us. If the KGB suddenly descended, the many-throated groan, the dying whisper of millions, the unspoken testament of those who had perished, would all be in their hands, and I would never be able to reconstruct it all, my brain would never be capable of it again.

I could have enjoyed myself so much, breathing the fresh air, resting, stretching my cramped limbs, but my duty to the dead permitted no such self-indulgence. They are dead. You are alive: Do your duty. The world must know *all about it*. . . .

I understand these ecstasies of despair, and I experience them myself. At such moments I am capable of crying out! But this is the question to ask: Am I crying out against the greatest evil? Cry out just once and perish for it—yes, if you have never seen anything so horrible in all your life. But I have seen and known many worse things—*Gulag* is entirely made up of them. Why do I not cry out about that? Our past fifty years consists of nothing else. Yet we are silent. To cry out now would be to deny the whole history of our country, to help in prettifying it must preserve my vocal cords for the *great* outcry! It will not be long now. Wait until they begin translating *Gulag* into English. . . .

A rationalization of cowardice? or a sensible argument?

I held my peace. From that moment I bore an additional weight on my back. At the time of Hungary I was nobody, and it didn't matter whether I cried out or not. Now it was Czechoslovakia—and I held my tongue. It was all the more shameful because I bore a special personal responsibility for Czechoslovakia. It is generally admitted that the whole thing *began* there with the Writers' Congress, and the congress began with Kohout reading my letter aloud.

There is only one way I shall ever be able to rid myself of this stain: and that is if my words someday start something else, this time in our own country. . . .

The [KGB] could take my children hostage—posing as "gangsters," of course. (They did not know that we had thought of this and made a superhuman decision: our children were no dearer to us than the memory of the millions done to death, and nothing could make us stop that book.) . . .

There is no weighing these things in the scales of reason: If you find something scorching your soles—find the ground like a frying pan under your feet—you'll dance, all right! You feel ashamed to be a mere historical novelist when people are being strangled before your eyes. I should not think much of the author of *Gulag* if he preserved a diplomatic silence about its continuation into the present. For our intelligentsia, the internment of Zhores Medvedev in a loony bin held greater dangers and raised larger issues than what had happened to Czechoslovakia. It was a noose around our own throats. So I decided to write something. I began my first drafts very menacingly:

"WARNING!"

(To *all of them*, all the torturers. I am very apt to be carried away at first, but then I recover my self-control.) During my time in the camps I had got to know the enemies of the human race quite well: they respect the *big fist* and nothing else; the harder you slug them, the safer you will be. (People in the West simply will not understand this, and are forever hoping to mollify them with concessions.) As soon as I rubbed the sleep out of my eyes in the morning I longed to get to my novel, but the urge to rewrite my Warning just once more would be too strong for me, I was so worked up about it. By the fifth draft it had become rather milder: "THE WAY WE LIVE. . . ."

Lambs-wool Hairdos under Arc Lights

I gave the [Swedish] Academy [who had awarded me the Nobel Prize for literature] three days to receive my letter and act upon it. I intended to release it through samizdat at the end of the third day. But the Academy sent a telegram saying that it wanted to make the letter public only at the banquet. That would be too late for me. I needed to make it clear *immediately* that I was not going. But the Swedes were not to experience the explosive power of Russian samizdat: the contents of the letter trickled through their own fingers, probably while it was being translated into Swedish, and they sent me a second telegram in hot pursuit of the first: they apologized, deplored the leak, and asked me to send something else for the banquet.

I had not been intending to. I had said the little I wanted to say for the time being, measuring my words, and all that really mattered would go into my lecture. But the telegram set me off again.

It had not been part of my plan, but why not take a paragraph that had dropped out of my Nobel lecture and use it here, making the coincidence in dates my excuse.

"Your Majesty! Ladies and gentlemen! I cannot overlook the remarkable fact that the day on which the Nobel Prizes are being presented coincides with International Human Rights Day. . . ."

(Gentlemen—your Scythian guest is disappointed in you. Why all those lambs-wool hairdos under the arc lights? Why is a white tie *de rigueur* and a camp jerkin not allowed? And what strange custom is this—to listen to the speech in which a laureate sums up his work, his whole life, with food before you? How abundantly the tables are laden, how sumptuous are the dishes, how casually you pass them, as though you saw them every day. Serve yourselves, chew your food, wash it down . . . but what of the writing on the

157

wall, in letters of fire—"Mene, mene, tekel, upharsin." Do you not see it . . . ?)

The Word as Weapon

It is infinitely difficult to begin when mere words must move a great block of inert matter. But there is no other way if none of the material is strength on your side. And a shout in the mountains has been known to start an avalanche. . . .

Books are like divisions or army corps: at times they must dig themselves in, hold their fire, lie low; at times they just cross bridges in the dark and noiselessly; at times, concealing their preparations to the last dribble of loose earth, they must rush into a concerted offensive from the least expected quarter at the least expected moment. While the author is like a commander in chief, here throwing in a unit, there moving up another to wait its turn. . . .

Calling and Conscience

Later the true significance of what had happened would inevitably become clear to me, and I would be numb with surprise. I have done many things in my life that conflicted with the great aims I had set myself—and something has always set me on the true path again. I have become so used to this, come to rely on it so much, that the only task I need to set myself is to interpret as clearly and quickly as I can each major event in my life.

(V. V. Ivanov came to the same conclusion, though life supplied him with quite different material to think about. He puts it like this: "Many lives have a mystical sense, but not everyone reads it aright. More often than not it is given to us in cryptic form, and when we fail to decipher it, we despair because our lives seem meaningless. The secret of a great life is often a man's success in deciphering the mysterious symbols vouchsafed to him, understanding them and so learning to walk in the true path.")

. . . I was disgusted with myself. The most terrible danger of all is that you may do violence to your conscience, sully your honor. No threat of physical destruction can compare with it. . . .

In retrospect, almost all my life since the day I was first arrested had been the same: just for *that* particular week, *that* month, *that* season, *that* year, there had always been some reason for not writing—it was inconvenient or dangerous or I was too busy—always some need to postpone it. If I had given in to common sense, once, twice, ten times, my achievement as a writer would have been incomparably smaller. But I had gone on writing—as a bricklayer, in overcrowded prison huts, in transit jails without so much as a pencil, when I was dying of cancer, in an exile's hovel after a double teaching shift. I had let nothing—dangers, hindrances, the need for rest—interrupt my writing, and only because of that could I say at fifty-five that I now had no more than twenty years of work to get through, and had put the rest behind me. . . .

The one worrying thing was that I might not be given time to carry out the whole scheme. I felt as though I was about to fill a space in the world that was meant for me and had long awaited me, a mold, as it were, made for me alone, but discerned by me only this very moment. I was a molten substance, impatient, unendurably impatient, to pour into my mold, to fill it full, without air bubbles or cracks, before I cooled and stiffened. . . .

Once again, my vision and my calculations are probably faulty. There are many things which I cannot see even at close quarters, many things in which the Hand of the Highest will correct me. But this casts no cloud over my feelings. It makes me happier, more secure, to think that I do not have to plan and manage everything for myself, that I am only a sword made sharp to smite the unclean forces, an enchanted sword to cleave and disperse them.

Grant, O Lord, that I may not break as I strike! Let me not fall from Thy hand!

Conclusion

How simply it is all ending. The calf has butted and butted the oak. The pygmy would stand up to Leviathan. Till the world press fulminated: ". . . the only Russian whom the regime fears! He is undermining Marxism—and he walks around central Moscow a free man!"

. . . All my life I had been tortured by the impossibility of speaking the truth aloud. My whole life had been spent in hacking my way to an open space where I could tell the truth in public. Now, at last, I was free, as I had never been before, no axe was poised above my head, and dozens of microphones belonging to the world's most important press agencies were held out toward my lips. Say something! It would indeed be unnatural not to say something! Now I could make the weightiest pronouncements, and they would be carried far and wide, to the ends of the earth. . . . But inside me something had snapped. Perhaps because I had been transplanted so quickly that I hadn't even had time to decide how I felt about it, let alone to prepare a speech. That was part of it. But there was something more. I suddenly felt that I would demean myself if I indulged in abuse from a distance, if I spoke out where everyone speaks out, where speaking out is permitted. The words came out of their own accord:

"I said quite enough while I was in the Soviet Union. Now I shall be silent for a while. . . ."

I have never doubted that the truth would be restored to my people. I believe that we shall repent, that we shall be spiritually cleansed, that the Russian nation will be reborn.